Words

Traditions in Linguistics

Revised

EL MOUATAMID BEN ROCHD

Words

Traditions in Linguistics

Revised

© 2020, El Mouatamid Ben Rochd

Edition: BoD – Books on Demand,
12/14 rond-point des Champs Élysées, 75008 Paris
Impression : BoD - Books on Demand, Norderstedt, Allemagne

ISBN : 9782322242603

Dépot legal: octobre 2020

To Patrick Griffiths

ACKNOWLEDGMENT

Many thanks to Dr El Heggach, Dr Chaouch, Bob Quinn, Mohamed Touhami and Soumia Ben Rochd.

CONTENTS

PREFACE		17
INTRODUCTION		19
1.	Philosophy	21
2.	Psychology	22
3.	Language	22
4.	Phonetics	24
5.	Phonology	25
6.	Morphology	27
7.	Syntax	28
8.	Semantics	31
9.	Sociolinguistics	32
10.	The best language?	33
JAPANESE TRADITION		35
1.	The History of Japan	35
2.	Phonetics & phonology	36
3.	The History of Linguistics in Japan	38
4.	The Linguistic Thought in Japan	39
5.	50 Sounds Chart	40
6.	The Writing System	40
7.	Japanese Syntax	40

CHINESE TRADITION		43
1.	Chinese Language	43
2.	Metalinguistic Speculation	44
3.	Lexicography	45
4.	Phonology	45
5.	Twentieth Century Developments	45
PANINI		49
ARISTOTLE (384-322 BC)		53
1.	Truth	53
2.	The Ten Categories	54
3.	Proposition	55
4.	Contradiction	56
5.	Syllogism	57
6.	Conditionals	58
HEBREW TRADITION		61
1.	History	61
2.	Theology	64
3.	Language	64
ARABIC TRADITION (I): SIBAWAIHI		71
1.	Introduction	71
2.	Sound System	72
	2.1. Sound Outlets	72
	2.2. Distinctive Features	72
	2.3. Phonological Processes	73
3.	Non-Concatenative Morphology	73

| 4. | Transformational Syntax | 74 |

ARABIC TRADITION (II): IBN JINNI — 77

.1	Arabic	77
2.	Arabic and Islam	77
3.	The Structure of Arabic	78
4.	Life	78
5.	Books	79
6.	Theories	80
7.	Semantics	81

BERBER TRADITION — 83

1.	Introduction	83
2.	History	84
3.	Language	86
3.1.	Verb Morphology in Tarifit	86
3.2.	Ouhalla's Syntactic Theories	87
3.3.	Susi Idioms	89

GERMAN TRADITION — 91

1.	Germany	91
2.	Goethe	91
3.	German	92

GRIMM'S LAW: A REVIEW OF THE KING JAMES VERSION — 95

.1	The Bible	95
.2	English	96
3.	Grimm's Law	97

4. Idioms	100
SAUSSURE (I)	101
SAUSSURE (II) : COURS DE LINGUISTIQUE GÉNÉRALE	113
1. Life and Books of Ferdinand de Saussure (1857-1913)	113
2. Saussure's Contributions in Linguistics and his Influence on Linguists' Thought	114
DANISH TRADITION	117
FUNCTIONALISM	123
1. Prague	123
2. London	132
3. Robert Le Page	140
WITTGENSTEIN	143
MARXISM & MARRISM	151
BLOOMFIELDIANS	153
1. Bloomfield	153
2. Sapir-Whorf	154
3. Zellig Harris	155
PIKE (I): SUMMARY OF PIKE'S *LINGUISTIC CONCEPTS – AN INTRODUCTION TO TAGMEMICS* (1982)	157
1. The Observer and Things	158
1.1. Theory	158
1.2. Survey of Tagmemic Theory	160
1.3. Particles	161
1.4. Wave	162
1.5. Field	163

2.	The Unit		164
	2.1.	Contrast and Identification	164
	2.2.	Variation	165
	2.3.	Distribution	166
3.	Hierarchy		167
	3.1.	Grammatical Hierarchy	167
	3.2.	The Phonological Hierarchy	168
	3.3.	The Referential Hierarchy	168
4.	Context		170
	4.1.	Form and Meaning	170
	4.2.	Sharing as Prerequisite to Change	171
	4.3.	Universe of Discourse	172

PIKE (II): SUMMER INSTITUTE OF LINGUISTICS [SIL]   175

1.	Life	175
2.	The 'emic'/ 'etic' Theory	176
3.	Tagmemics Theory	176
4.	Pike and Religion	177

LABOV'S SOCIOLINGUISTICS   179

CHOMSKY'S TG GRAMMAR   183

1.	Chomsky's Life		183
2.	Phrase Structure Grammar		184
3.	Transformational Grammar		187
4.	Standard Theory		189
	4.1.	Phrase Structure Rules & Lexicon	189
	4.2.	Transformations	192

	4.3.	Transformational Cycle	194
5.		Pronominalization	195
6.		Conclusions	196

LANGACKER'S COGNITIVE GRAMMAR	197
CHILD LANGUAGE	201

1.		Overview	201
2.		Searle's Taxonomy	202
3.		Patrick Griffiths	205

PSYCHOLINGUISTICS	209
CONCLUSION	221
GLOSSARY	223
BIBLIOGRAPHY	235

PREFACE

Einstein once said, 'it's a miracle if you don't see a miracle in everything.' So, obviously LANGUAGE is a miracle, if not the miracle of miracles. It is such a wonderful miracle that is has attracted the attention of many, such as early Greek philosophers like Plato and Aristotle, and modern philosophers like Austin and Wittgenstein. They all tried to capture the nature of this 'miracle' by giving it acceptable – reasonable – definitions. Some have succeeded, to some extent, in their endeavour and some have only "lured the fly into the bottle!" (Wittgenstein)

Man has been given the secret/power to assign symbols to referents e.g. different places (Paris, NY), people (Jesus, Marx), concrete objects (tree, table) and abstract concepts (freedom, justice). By naming these, man has been able to connect utterances to objects in the real world. This has a tremendous importance for man. We can appreciate its value only by imagining a world without language: the extreme difficulty to keep life going on, if we did not have this semiotic power; the hardship of communication and bitterness of people's interrelations. We would have to bring about the thing itself that we want to talk about in front of our eyes, say a tree, or go to the Himalaya Mountains, or have to bring the person we want to talk about. This would have been a tremendous hardship next to impossible. Each nation is keen on preserving its culture and language as part and parcel, if not the hub, of that culture; so each nation has produced bright scholors to deal with it, from the Far East, the Middle East, Europe and finally America; all contributed from antiquity, the Middle Ages, the Renaissance and the Modern Times.

Starting from the nineteenth century, language has become the field of research of the specialists, viz. philologists such as Paul and Schleicher, and more recently – modern linguists, such as Saussure, Bloomfield and Noam Chomsky (in the western tradition).

The more than 3.000 languages spoken in the world nowadays can be seen as just one coin with two faces 'sound/sense' or 'signifiant/signifié' (Saussure, 1916), 'deep/surface structures' (Chomsky 1967), or simply the matching of 'expression and meaning.' The components of language have been studied scientifically by the specialists of phonetics (Henry Sweet), morphology (Leonard Bloomfield), syntax (Noam Chomsky), semantics (Aristotle) and pragmatics (Charles Pierce). Each discipline is a man's life consumer. It is indeed as big as the earth!

INTRODUCTION

'Why study language, in the first place?' you may ask.

To answer this question, I may quote Noam Chomsky's answer to Dr Mazen Al-Waer: "When someone introduces himself in a party as a doctor, people will wonder in which hospital he works, and when somebody introduces himself as a lawyer, everybody will think when he has a legal problem, the lawyer would be able to help. But when you introduce yourself as a linguist people will be astonished and ask what do you mean by linguistics? And when you try to explain to them that linguistics is a scientific study of languages, they will say, 'well, why do you bother and study languages since we speak them naturally?' Do you think that linguistics can change people's opinions one day, and do you think the study of linguistics is important?"

Chomsky: "In our own intellectual tradition going back to the Greeks it has always been assumed, and I think correctly, that the most important topic to study is the human being, the question what is the nature of humans, and in particular, how the human mind works. There can hardly be a more significant topic for investigation for us than the human mind and how it functions. The most interesting aspects of the human mind are those intellectual achievements that are carried out naturally, that seem so obvious to us that we cannot even see at first that there is a problem to be studied. The first difficulty that you have to overcome if you want to study human beings is to try to attain a sense of wonder and surprise at the fact that you are able to do what you are able to do normally. If you do not think about it, it seems obvious that you just talk and say what is on your mind. But the question is: how are you able to do this? What is about the child that makes it possible for the child to acquire this ability but does not make it possible for *an ape or a dog* [italics mine] or any other organism to acquire this ability? What is this capacity? What underlies it? What are its properties? What are its features?"

The psychologist, Wolfgang Kohler, once remarked that it is necessary to develop a kind of "*psychic distance*" [italics mine] from the acts that you perform naturally. You have to be able to look at them as it were from the outside, to recognize how amazing they are, before you can begin to try to find out what are the capacities on which these acts are based. It is not a problem when you study, say, physics, since we are studying something that is external to us, we already have psychic distance. We do not move the planets so therefore the fact that the planets move already seems remarkable. But since we are the ones who are doing the speaking, what we are doing sometimes does not seem remarkable, but rather somewhat obvious. However, it is really much more remarkable than the fact that the planets are moving the way they are."

(Mazen Al-Waer, 'An Interview with American Linguist Noam Chomsky', Dept. of Linguistics and Philosophy. MIT. 1980).

1. Philosophy

The ultimate goal of philosophers has always been the pursuit of TRUTH. But usually, they (and people in general) disagree about what is true and what is false [cf. Shakespeare's "wisdom"]. In Europe alone, there were indeed big and bitter intellectual fights, in the Middle Ages, about the sources of (true) knowledge to begin with. Some said it should be ecclesiastic (Martin Luther/Pike), others opted for rational (Decartes/Chomsky), still others for empiricist (Francis Bacon/Bloomfield) sources. The Pope in Rome, Martin Luther and Hegel represent the first trend. French René Descartes (*Discours de la méthode*) represents the second [cf. Deists]. English Roger Bacon is considered to be the pioneer of the last one (followed by Francis Bacon's *Novum Organum*).

There are, at least, three levels of influence of philosophy on linguistics, viz. 'ideological umbrella', epistemology and (more specifically) linguistic theory. The first one – ideology [cf. Marr] or religion [cf. Pike] – concerns the linguist as much as the layman in a given society. It is a sort of general umbrella that covers all members of a given society. Epistemology [theory of knowledge] touches the scientist – whatever his specialty may be; as each researcher is busy digging his own (narrow) field not knowing how to situate himself vis-à-vis other scientists. Epistemology will help him find his position and his relation with researchers in neighboring disciplines.

The last level of philosophical influence on linguistics is found in linguistic theorizing. After observation and many experiments, the linguist, like all other scientists, opts for the construction of general theories – using reason and logic. He is actually philosophizing (cf. PhD).

2. Psychology

Many people believe that the structure of language and its general features are universal and are deeply embedded in the human mind. At any rate, the human body displays an amazing organic unity synchronized and harmonized by God. Without signals from the nervous system no air would escape from the throat to produce speech sounds. So no separation is possible between speech, biology and physiology, nor is it possible to separate them from the ideas which are shaped by speaking.

Language is closely linked to psychology. In the 19th and early 20th centuries, language had soon attracted the attention of American psychologists such as Watson and Skinner (*Verbal Behaviour*), among others. They were the representatives of the Bahaviourist School of psychology in the US in the 50s. They were themselves influenced by the works of Russian biologist Pavlov [see glossary]. The latter is the initiator of 'stimulus-response' brain mechanism. He used dogs for his experiments.

By opposition to this school, Chomsky's innate theory suggests that *the human child is unique* as he comes to life preprogrammed for language acquisition. Chomsky seems to have revived Plato's notion of 'prenatal life' [see Psycholinguistics].

3. Language

Language is a conscious articulated means of communication shared by a speech community. It is, I believe, the best thing that the human being has been given. Thanks to it, we can speak about Chicago while we are thousands of miles far from it. We can also write about Moses while living in the 21st century. Without language, we would have to bring the Atlas chain right here, or at least go to Morocco if we want to point to those huge mountains. But, thanks to language, the distances, both in time and space are magically shortened.

Man communicates with his own species and with the other living creatures using a large set of different means. He can communicate his happiness, his anger, his excitement... by smiling, frowning, whistling, by gestures... or by the use of language, which is the best and the most sophisticated medium. Simply by using the air of his lungs, man can, tacitly, control his breathing and produce different organized and meaningful stretches of sounds.

Language use is shared by all (normal) human beings. Among the intellectuals, it is used by the man of letters to express his feelings in beautiful articulated forms. It is used by the philosopher to shape ideas and doctrines. It is used by the scientist to describe what he observes from the constituents of nature.

Now scientists are divided into many specialties, among which we find chemistry, medicine, physics, astronomy... and linguistics. All of them need language. For the linguist language knows a kind of reflexive reality. He uses language to describe language. The linguist is a scientist both rationally and empirically. He attempts to describe language by explicit formal means.

His objective and systematic approach applies on several levels: phonetics and phonology for the study of the speech sounds, morphology and syntax for the patterns, semantics and pragmatics for meaning; not to forget the psychological, historical and stylistic dimensions of language.

4. Phonetics

We may imagine language as a semi-conscious (we think about what to say but not about how to speak) string of sounds originating in an air chamber (lungs, glottis, mouth) by an initiator and passing through a particular shape of the oral cavity.

The speech sounds can be viewed within three dimensions: the place of articulation (lips, teeth…), the manner of articulation (stop, fricative…), and the presence versus absence of voice (vibration of the vocal cords). They can vary in a very large way; following a *'faisseau de traits pertinents'* (distinctive features) and this fact shows the tremendous ability of the speech organs which allow the production of a large set of sounds.

The most important parts of the oral tract are the *tongue*, the lips, the uvula, the glottis and the lungs. The speech sound is an acoustic wave carried by the air from the mouth of the speaker to the ear of the hearer; the lungs being the main air chamber. This air has to go first through the glottis, in which it comes across the best 'musical' strings of the world; or ligaments called 'vocal cords'. Further up, it may go to the nasal cavity if the uvula is lowered producing nasal sounds [m], [n], [ŋ], [ɲ] or 'color' other sounds like the French vowels [ɛ], [ɔ], and [a] which then become [ɛ̃], [ɔ̃], and [ã].

The air stream, however, goes mainly through the mouth and finds there the predominant speech organ which is the tongue – a very mobile muscle and the principle shaper of the oral tract. The speech sounds have been divided into two main categories: contoids and vocoids. The contoids are mostly stops [b], [t], [d],… and fricatives [ʒ], [ʃ],… The first ones stop the air for a moment before releasing it out of the mouth; the second ones narrow its space and cause its turbulence. The rest of the sounds are voiced and are subdivided according to a front-back dimension and a low-high one, representing their place of the hump of the tongue in the oral cavity.

The speech sound can be a stop, a fricative or a nasal. Each sound has many characteristics that differentiate it from the others. Sounds also vary in space and time. Not all of them are used in a single language; and throughout history, some are acquired and some are lost unlike the phonological system which persists relatively longer.

Phoneticians have come to draw a crucial distinction between articulatory phonetics, auditory phonetics and acoustic phonetics. Linguists are mainly concerned with the first.

5. Phonology

Many physiologically possible sounds are found in none of the known languages. Sound systems differ from language to language and there is no complete analogy between the sounds of different languages. One of the facts that betray non-native speakers.

Each language uses its share from the universal speech repertoire according to its particular sound system. The sounds behave differently in different linguistic environments of speech communities, of dialects or even idiolects. The reason why we recognize the voice of a speaker on the phone.

Some sounds like [X], [ɣ], [ʕ] are used by Arabic speakers but not by French and English speakers, while [θ] and [ð] are used by both Arabic and English people but not by the French. [p/b] and [f/v] are respectively distinctive in French (*pain* vs. *bain*, *feu* vs. *voeux*) and English, but [b] and [f] alone exist in Arabic. English has no [ʒ] in initial position of words (unless borrowed from another language). French has no [dʒ] while Arabic has no [ʒ].

Phonology is sometimes called phonemics because it is centered around the concept of the phoneme (minimal unit of sound capable of distinguishing words of different meanings (cf. Bloomfield). The English word 'man' contains three phonemes. It can be contrasted to 'ban', 'men' and 'map'.

Some segmental features like voice [pin/bin], length [read/read [past]) change the meaning of the words (minimal pairs). Velarization can also be phonemic. In Arabic for instance [t] and [tˤ] give a minimal pair [tiːn] (i.e. fig) and [tˤiːn] (i.e. clay), whereas in other languages they are merely allophones. Still in Arabic, we do not start with a consonant cluster and never end a word with a vowel.

Some stops like [q], [tˤ], [b], [dʒ], [d], have to be glottalized in order to be heard in final position. There are also some non-phonemic assimilations like the use of [u] which is deleted when it occurs before one of the following phonemes [j], [r], [m], [l], [ŭ], [n] and colored (doubled) before, [s], [ð], [θ], [k], [dʒ], [ʃ], [q], [s], [d], [tˤ], [z], [f], [t], [ ], [ ], or substituted for by [m], before [b] (this rule happens in French as well).

English is well known for its stress and intonation systems which affect (the) meaning, for instance *'English teacher vs. English 'teacher.* The phrasal verb 'to run up' is either 'the waiter [ran up the Bill]' (made the total), or 'the waiter ran [up the hill]'. Intonation distinguishes also questions, orders, statements: falling pitch e.g. in *'eh bien!'* meaning pity (in French), whereas the rising one means anger in *'Eh alors?'* When you have stepped on the toe of a French person.

It is the task of phonology to study the meaningful differences that exist in the phonetic data. It is also its task to discover the combination rules that make the words and utterances of a given language.

6. Morphology

The phoneme alone is not an independent linguistic unit as it has no meaning. We could accept it on the fringes of language; 'n!' could mean 'yes!'

Phonemes cannot, generally speaking, stand alone; so they are grouped into morphemes in order to be meaningful. There are free morphemes in English like 'open', 'table', etc. and bound morphemes like 'ed' and 's' (that the students usually forget!) which have grammatical functions but cannot occur alone. They express past and plural respectively. The plural and the past forms can be also realized by other devices as in 'men' and 'sang'.

The morphology of a word may express endless functions. For instance the use of the prefixes un-/dis- gives the negation of a word, e.g. un-able, dis-able-ed; the adjunction of the suffix -ly to an adjective gives an adverb, e.g. nice-ly.

In Arabic, the three consonantal stem expresses a verbal entity and is sometimes provided by a diacritical system of vowels (*harakat*). The inflection /a/ gives the past tense; /at/ gives the feminine, /ja/ gives the present, the initial /ʔ/ gives a category of plural when coordinated with an infix /aa/ ʔatfaal, ʔabqaar, ʔaqsaam...

Another dimension of morphology is compounding, e.g. wind-mill, white-board, face-cloth, etc.

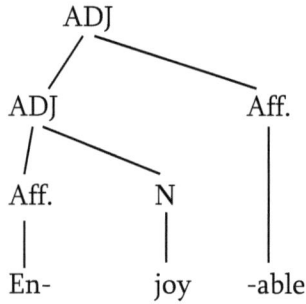

Morphology deals with the internal structure of the word (Bloomfield), while syntax deals with the internal structure of the sentence.

7. Syntax

Neither phoneme nor morpheme is enough for the study of the structure of language. Language must be approached syntactically as well. The linguist must show the recurrent elements and the recurrent patterns both on the categorial side NP, VP, Det... and on the functional one S V O. The linear structure of language presents the sentence as its upper limit. It is isolated in speech by pauses and a particular intonation. It is distinguished from the other sentences – in the written language – by the punctuation (full stop, exclamation mark, etc...). The sentence usually consists of a series of words and could be considered as the ideal utterance. An utterance like 'going home?' can convey the same meaning as 'Are you going home?' but it is not a complete sentence.

Each sentence is meaningful when it is placed in its right context. And again word order is essential, at least in English and French, because each sentence form corresponds to one type of meaning. The sentence *Jean a aperçu le loup* is different from *le loup a aperçu Jean*.

    1   2   3   vs.   3   2   1

In an inflectional language like Arabic, however, order is merely stylistic. Although the primary sentence pattern is VSO:

ʔakala Ali alXubza.

Ate Ali the-bread.

The inflections determine the subject, the verb and the object allowing structures like SVO.

Ali ʔakala lXubza.

Or even VOS.

ʔibtalaa Ibraahiima rabbu-hu (the Holy Quran)

Tested Abraham his-Lord

The sentence is essentially made up of words. The words present a peculiar grammatical stability which can be clashed against by other stretches like the quantifier 'all', in the sentences:

All children played games.

*Children all played games.

Children played all games.

* Children played games all. (pidgin)

The words can be separated in speech by a pause. They can stand alone but do not permit any internal rearrangement (at least in English and French). The word has a unique behaviour and is the 'minimum free form' (as Leonard Bloomfield put it).

Series of words form regular patterns. The sentence '(last night) (my friend) (came home) (late)' can be chopped into (last night) (my friend came home) (late)'. These parts can be replaced respectively by (yesterday or last Saturday), (he or John), (ate or slept), (quickly or early) yesterday, he ate quickly.

Each item can be replaced by another one from the same class of words, leaving the patterns unchanged. This is in fact the clue to learning a language and understanding it. Within the sentence, the words or the phrases are organized according to three syntactic relations. The first one is the positional relation, which allows a sentence like: 'Ali bought a car' but not '*car bought Ali'.

The second syntactic relation is called co-occurrence. It permits 'Ali bought a car' (because it belongs to classes of words that conform to the selectional rules like [+human, -common] but does not allow 'green ideas sleep'. The third syntactic relation is substitution. The sentence structure is kept while the items are substituted for by others from the same category. 'Ali bought a car' can become 'he bought a car', 'Ali bought it', 'he bought it'.

For Transformational-Generative grammar there is a fourth syntactic relation. It relates sentences (by rearranging their structure). For instance, 'Ali bought a car' is related to: 'A car was bought by Ali', 'Did Ali buy a car?' 'Ali did not buy a car'. It predicts possible sentences by expanding the deep structure into the lexical and grammatical items of different sentences. It finally distinguishes ambiguous sentences, such as 'Old men and women', which means either: old [men and women] or [old men] and women.

TG has also shown that the items of the sentence are organized in a grammatical hierarchy, (each node dominating what is below it) and that there is an underlying basic form for sentences, which is universal and innate.

8. Semantics

Language is, actually, a mere system of symbols (Ferdinand de Saussure) used to convey meaning. It is a system of arbitrary 'signifiers' related – as Saussure put it – to 'signified'.

The phonological and syntactic aspects of language are essentially directed towards meaning. Each word has its own entailments and the addition of the entailments of the words of a sentence form the entailments of this sentence e.g. 'my friend came' entails 'he came', 'a man came', 'a man did something', 'something happened'.

Meaning remains, however, vague and many syntactically well-formed sentences are meaningless; like the famous one given by Chomsky: 'colourless green ideas sleep furiously!'

On the other hand, there is no clear relation between form and meaning, nor any strong relation between language and logic; *musajjala* which means recorded in Arabic is used for 'recorder'. *'Si jamais tu le trouves'*, *'jamais'* – meaning never – is here put for 'when': 'When you meet him'.

There is no easy answer in semantics because every utterance is connected to a particular context, to the free will and meaning given to it by the speaker, and finally to the whole human experience and knowledge. We also not only speak about things but give direct or indirect judgements about them as well.

Polemic disputes often arise about the meaning of words like democracy, civilization, primitive... what is good and what is bad, but "to say that this is bad and this is good" – as African journalist Babs Fafunbwa put it – is simply to play God!

9. Sociolinguistics

The individual with his complex organization and complex behaviour is still bound to live within a society and have social relations; which makes things more complex. Language uses are many. It primarily helps the individual in communicating with his social group. He does not express what is taken for granted by the community or what is classified by the speech context. He does not always express what he means nor means what he expresses. 'Hi!' is used by friends instead of saying: 'Good morning Madam!' 'Cheers!' is used between middle class people in GB instead of 'Good bye madam!' 'Good bye Sir!', *'Comment va?'* Or shortly *'ça va?'* instead of *'Comment allez-vous, Monsieur?'*

The social usage of words is in many ways tyrannical. First, because of the possible lack of communication between interlocutors, like the case described by Harold Pinter in his play *The Caretaker*. Second, by the exclusivity of some geographical and cultural contexts. A French man who wants *'gagner son pain'* (literally win his bread) in China is irrelevant (the Chinese eat rice!) as well as when he wants *'se faire une place au soleil'* in the desert! Third, the speech of an individual 'betrays' him before the human community. The class difference emphasized by the language awareness (cf. Le Page) is rather bitter. It remains however less so than the case of Pidgin/Creole speakers of colonized countries. Fourth, language can affect or even harm the economy of a country.

Belgium and Morocco, to take the examples of these two countries, have to print everything in two languages: French and Flemish, and French and Arabic, respectively.

Language is also linked to politics. Those who control language can claim to control people as well, state of things well described by George Orwell in his 'prophetic novel' *1984*.

Language is always (excluding the thinking aloud case) uttered within a speech community. The contexts are many and all depends on who is saying what, to whom, where and when, because the type of language used bears the identity of the speaker and the culture of the community or group he is identified with.

10. The best language?

Is it Arabic, English, French, Chinese, Sanskrit Sumerian or Babylonian?

There is a big linguistic war for determining which language is the best. Describing French, French Diderot (1751) states, *'notre langue sera celle de la vérité, si jamais elle revient sur terre, et… la grecque, la romaine et les autres seront les langues de la fable et du mensonge.'* (Our language will be the language of truth, if it could come back on earth, and Greek, Roman and the others will be the language of fables and falsehood). Nowadays, there is a bitter war between *'Francophonie'* and Anglophony.

An Indian friend of mine insisted that 'Sanskrit is the first language ever!'

English Muslim Abdel Haq Bewly states, 'Allah (T) picked out the Arabic language for his final revelation to the tribe of

Adam. He could have chosen any place and any tongue...' According to William Wright, Arabic has preserved a higher degree of likeness to the original Semitic language. German philosopher of the 17th c. Leibniz "firmly placed Hebrew within the Arabic family" [viz. considered Arabic to be the mother of Hebrew] (Robins 1980, p. 167), and so does the Israeli Academy. American Michael Hart states that 'the centrality of the Koran in the Moslem religion and the fact that it is written in Arabic have probably prevented the Arab language from breaking up into mutually unintelligible dialects, which might otherwise have occurred in the intervening thirteen centuries.' Chomsky in his Minimalist Program considers Arabic a 'suggestive case." (Chomsky 1995, p. 199)

JAPANESE TRADITION

Like other cognitive linguists, I believe that language and culture (including history and religion) are like a glass of milk. You cannot do with one without the other. To know the culture of a people you have to study their language, and vice versa, to study their language is a key to understanding their culture.

Popular "Clichés" about Japan are Sushi, Sumo, Judo, Aikido, Katana, Samurai... and Nagasaki... Linguistically, Japanese syllable is canonical (CV) and sentences always end with the verb. In fact Japan is much more than that. The sense of respect and politeness of the Japanese people is proverbial, to mention but this one nice aspect of their culture.

1. The History of Japan

The history of Japan goes a long way back to the Neolithic period (5000-300BC) with its fishing, hunting, pottery and Shinto traditions. The protohistoric period saw the coming of the Chinese influence (300BC-300AD) with the rice agriculture and iron work. The 1st c. saw the introduction of Buddhism (538) from China through Korea. In the 6th c., the emperor (son of goddess Amaterasu) ruled in a feudal system. Then came the Shugun (1603-1867) with Edo (future Tokyo) as the capital and the unity of Japan thanks to Tokugawa, a Shinto priest. Japan was built on a rigid hierarchy and closed its doors to the external world. Japanese literature flourished. In 1854 the USA threaded and succeeded in opening Japan to its influence. With the coming of the Meiji revolution, Japan strived to catch up with the western superpower, which was successfully achieved. Japan became developed, powerful and… aggressive. It invaded and defeated its neighbors; China, Russia and Korea. In 1941 came the confrontation with rival America in Pearl Harbor, which, as a reaction, led to dreadful Hiroshima and Nagazaki bombings. Demilitarized modern Japan soon became the second economic power of the world.

2. Phonetics & phonology

There is usually a confusion concerning the difference between phonetics and phonology. Their duality seems, to many students, redundant or at least confusing. To simplify things, let us say that "phonetics" is the study of speech sounds, and their characteristics such as plosive, continuant, voiced, etc. Whereas phonology is the study of the rules that govern the speech sounds, such as assimilation, word boundaries (#), gemination. A later development in sound studies is prosodic phonology which studies prosody, mora, onset, etc.

In 1990, McCarthy suggested to develop Brame's approach to the phonology of Classical Arabic, by using his syllabic approach, which was meant to supersede both segmental morphology as well as Chomsky's feature based phonology. Segmental morphology would consider electric; with /k/ and electric with /s/ as two allomorphs. Feature-based phonology would "explain" this phenomenon by introducing the feature [back]; i.e. a back sound would become a minus back before a minus back sound. For McCarthy, this phenomenon, like others, must be explained using Templatic and/or Prosodic theory; based on the essential concept of "syllable." The syllable consists of a hierarchy. English word p-i-t for instance, consists of one syllable, the onset of which is /b/ and the rhyme of which is /it/, itself consisting of a nucleus; the vowel /i/: There is further a hierarchy of nuclei which is that of the sonorants [l, a, m, j, u, r, w, I, n]. It includes vowels, semivowels, liquids and nasals.

Sandhi

In Japanese, *sandhi* transformation consists of voicing the initial consonant of a morpheme e.g. *ka ga* in the middle of a word. While gemination of a consonant when not word-final e.g. *sho- issho ? gaku - gakku. Renjo.* A terminal n or q becomes n or m when derived from historical m or t. When the first syllable ends with /n/ it can undergo transformation.

Generally speaking, the syllable is a (mathematical) function of the segments. The sonorant hierarchy would determine the strength (S) and the weakness (W) of the segments of the syllable, with a correlation between these and stress assignment. Stress would fall on the strongest string. McCarthy further develops his idea to prove the viability – if not the superiority of his theory over those of his predecessors. He actually suggests two competing theories: Templatic morphology and Prosodic theory.

Prosodic hierarchy

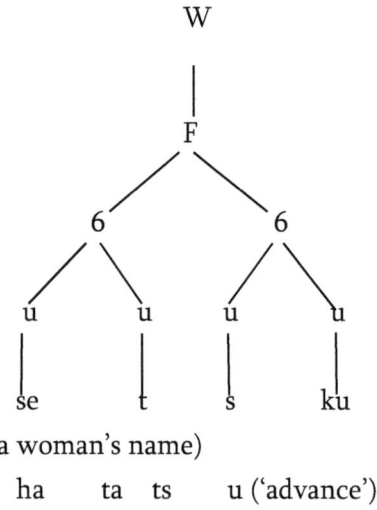

(a woman's name)
ha ta ts u ('advance')

The units of the prosodic hierarchy are the WORD, the FOOT, the SYLLABLE and the MORA (by definition heavy syllables (CVV, CVC) contain two moras while light syllables contain just one CV).

(Ben Rochd 2020b)

3. The History of Linguistics in Japan

According to Stefan Kaiser (1995), Japan is proud of its old ancestral scholarship but its linguistic studies lacked the leadership of a "Panini." Much influence in language (script) and religion came from neighboring China. Then an interest grew in German philology in the nineteenth century. Japanese linguistic thought went through three stages: early and medieval period, early modern period and modern period.

In the early and medieval period, the Japanese adopted the Chinese kanji system (4th c. AD) then turned it into a phonetic system (see Japanese complex morphology). Diglossia is also present in Japanese, as it distinguishes private from official forms. The early linguistic studies were carried out by Buddhist monks.

In the early period before the contact with Europe, morphology was the prime concern, with the emergence of Kokugogaku School. It was a secrecy teaching period. The modern period saw the emergence of the comparative approach and the establishment of Tokyo Imperial University by foreign scholars like English Chamberlain. One of his students Ueda (1867-1937) is considered as the father of Japanese linguistics. He had studied at Leipzig and introduced comparative linguistics to Japan (see Herman Paul) then Hattori, a structuralist who showed the failure of Western models to deal with the Japanese language, the Yoshi Yamada proposed a model proper to Japanese based on dichotomies: concept-relation words, *chinjutsuron* predication theory (subject-predicate vs. topic-comment). Japanese Phonology was influenced with Prague and American phonemics. Ueda dealt with dialectology, vocabulary, grammar and phonology of Japanese dialects. After World War II, many Japanese students came back from Europe and the US with the latest methodology.

4. The Linguistic Thought in Japan

Japanese scholars have always been keen on the study of Sanskrit and Chinese rhyme. During the Tang period (9th c.) the bulk of these studies was carried out by Japanese Shinto priests. They managed to preserve the Yunjing tables better than the Chinese themselves. Ultimately two syllabic method were devised to describe the phonetic system of Japanese, known as the Kana, together with a phonetic table which came to be known as *gojuon* 'fifty sounds' based on Indian phonetic studies.

5. 50 Sounds Chart

a ka ya sa ta na ra ha ma wa

i ki i si ti ni ri hi mi wi

u ku yu su tu nu ru hu mu u

e ke e se te ne re he me we

o ko yo so to no ro ho mo wo

6. The Writing System

The Japanese took their writing system from China. Since each Chinese character represents one word, it was hard to use it for a highly inflected language like Japanese. In the 8th c. AD, the Japanese started using the Chinese characters as phonetic symbols, one symbol for one syllable. By the 9th c., the Chinese characters were simplified to make up the syllabary system known as *Kana*. The other system was the *Katakana*, in which one part of a Chinese character stood for a phonetic symbol, and finally *Hiragana*. After World War II, the number of symbols was reduced to 1850. Nowadays, Japan has got three writing systems: *Hiragana* (46), *Katakana* (used for foreign names) and *Kanji* (50000 characters).

7. Japanese Syntax

Japanese is usually considered as belonging to SOV language typology. In fact, the only condition on sentence acceptability is that the verb should consistently occur sentence-finally, which logically leads for the following options:

- SOV
- OSV

Functional items such as particles identify the grammatical functions of the constituents of the Japanese sentence. Another prominent feature of Japanese syntax is the prominence of the Topic-Comment (theme-rhyme) structure.

Tanaka-san desu

"As for this person, (it) is Mr./Ms. Tanaka."

Another option is to indicate the topic of the sentence by particle *wa*:

kochira wa Tanaka san desu

"As for this person, (it) is Mr./Ms. Tanaka."

Kochira (this) is the topic of the sentence, indicated by the particle *wa*. The topic and the subject are not necessarily the same:

Zō wa hana ga nagai

"As for elephant(s), (the) nose(s) (is/are) long."

Zō (elephant) is the topic, while *hana* (nose) is the subject.

Japanese is a pro-drop language. It omits pronouns, as they can be deduced from preceding sentences. They, unlike their counterparts in other languages can also be modified by adjectives:

Odoroita kare wa michi o hashitte itta

"The amazed he ran down the street."

Adjectives usually play the role of predicators. In Japanese they can stand for a whole sentence:

Urayamashii!"

"(I am) jealous (of it)!"

Questions in Japanese have the same structure as affirmative sentences; the only differentiation is in intonation. Sometimes the question particle *–ka* is added, e.g. *Ii desu* (It is OK) becomes *Ii desu-ka* (Is it OK?). On other occasions *–no* can be added, e.g. *Dōshite konai-no?* (Why aren't (you) coming?)

Negative sentences are formed by inflecting the verb e.g. *Pan-o taberu* (I will eat bread) or (I eat bread) becomes *Pan-o-tebenai* (I will not eat bread) or (I do not eat bread.)

It is sometimes said that the Japanese never say "NO!" out of politeness.

Encyclodia Wilkpidia

Ben Rochd (2020b)

CHINESE TRADITION

When we speak about China, the first images that come to mind are President Mao Tse Tung, hard communism, millions of mouths to feed, the indoctrination of the Muslim minority and Corona. Actually, China is much more than that. It has one of the ancestral and most interesting cultures of the world, ranging from culinary arts, to calligraphy, medicine, martial arts (Kung Fu) and religions.

Geographically, China hosts the mighty Himalaya Mountains (8846 m), huge rivers Yang Zi (5980 km) and Huang He (Yellow River 4845 km), has more than a billion inhabitants, followers of Confucius (3rd c. BC) or Buddha (563 BC). It is known for its famous monuments such as the Great Wall, the Shaolin temple, the Silk Road, the mandarin clerks. China submitted many wars and foreign intrusions: the 1595 missionaries, the Opium War launched by the British in 1842, the war with Japan, the rise of the Chinese boxers who fought against the Russians, English, French and German colonizers, the tribulations and sufferings of the Long March. (Dictionnaire Encyclopedique)

1. Chinese Language

According to Wang Williams (1995), Chinese can be proud as it is 'of all the living languages of the world, the language that has the longest unbroken recorded history, with texts in the language dating from as long as 35 centuries, and there is reason to believe that the art of writing in China may go many centuries further back than this.' Still Chinese linguistics has no parallel in Europe or ancient India, due essentially to the nature of that language and to its script. It is a language of little inflection and no word movement, the script is more ideographic (direct representation) than phonetic. Ideology can also be brought in; after the religions of Buddhism and Confucianism, came communism with Maoism and its politics, claiming that the unity of a nation can only be achieved through a standardizing of its official language (Mandarin), at the expense of dialects and the languages of minorities, excluding their cultures and languages.

According to Wang Williams, the history of the Chinese tradition in linguistics can be divided into four stages: metalinguistic speculation, lexicography, dialect geography, phonology, the study of tone, work on language change, and psycholinguistics. Wang (1995) deals with metalinguistic speculation, lexicography, dialect geography, phonology, and says nothing about the rest.

2. Metalinguistic Speculation

The first Chinese linguist was Xun Zi (335 BC) who produced Zhen Ming 'Rectification of Names' a treaties done on the works of philosopher Confucius (551 BC). The words have no intrinsic truth in themselves but are given their truth-value by the users based on agreed social convention.

3. Lexicography

In the Zhou period (221 BC) the 'trip data collecting was carried out by Yang Xiong, who used to ask soldiers and officials coming from different parts of China about their dialects. The writing system was a hindrance to accuracy of such an approach that cannot reflect the differences in phonetic and sociolinguistic aspects.

4. Phonology

Ancient China can boast of its early expertise in acoustic studies and physiology of speech production. The discovery of 1978 showed a set of 65 bronze bells going back some 2500 years. They were struck in different points to produce different musical tones. In the 2nd c. BC, Ling Shu Jing produced a work on anatomy showing the functions of the speech organs: epiglottis, uvula, tongue and lips in general terms, which are metaphorically described as the 'doors of speech.'

5. Twentieth Century Developments

More recently, i.e. in the twentieth-century, to be more precise, we witness a hybrid phenomenon in Chinese linguistic studies. When Western approaches proved a failure, comparative studies were undertaken by linguists in China and the West. One such mutual win-win relation is found in phonology in which the segment CV was surpassed to consider suprasegmental features of tone. Many Chinese linguists were trained both in the West and in China mainland, Taiwan and Hong Kong! It ended up with the creation of the first International Association of Chinese Linguistics in 1991.

According to Sampson (1980), 'if a race as intelligent as the Chinese can manage with a language which, in its historical period at least, has been near the isolating extreme, then how can we know that MAN needed to develop inflecting languages in order to realize his intellectual potential?'

According to Gleason (1969), 'the most extensive language family in eastern Asia is the Sino-Tibetan. It may be considered as containing two branches, Tibeto-Burman and Chinese.' From the European standpoint, Chinese has certain 'exotic' linguistic features:

- While English contrasts minimal pairs by the presence vs. absence of voice as in *pit* vs. *bit* (phonemic), a different possibility is found in Chinese that makes the contrast rest on the difference in aspiration. This is the case in many Chinese dialects.

- Objects are noted as singular or plural only when the speaker judges the information relevant. Number has a significant function in English grammar, whereas Chinese has a grammatical system in which number has no such part.

- Many written languages have large numbers of homonyms (*row* vs. *row*). English is only modestly equipped with such pairs. Literary Chinese, however, has many more.

- The Chinese writing system is generally assumed to have developed from pictorial representations. Graphemes and morphemes pose a problem. 'Some of the signs probably went through a stage of rather loosely defined reference to content rather than expression before each became tied to some specific morpheme.'

- The alphabetic system for Chinese does not indicate the pitches.
- For some reason (?) the Japanese have adapted the Chinese characters ().

PANINI

Panini was an ancient Indian grammarian. He was born in "Shalatula" in 520 BC in a town near "Attock" (in present-day Pakistan). Panini's work on grammar has had a great influence on scholarship in India and abroad. He played an enormous role in the development of Sanskrit grammar, but more generally on linguistic research in its broad sense. American linguist Leonard Bloomfield wrote in his book *Language,* qualifying him as: "one of the greatest monuments of human intelligence." Chomsky himself links his generative approach to that of Panini (*Aspects*).

Panini worked on the Sanskrit language essentially, using empirical methods. Sanskrit is the classical and religious language of the Indian Hindus. By way of illustration, Sanskrit means "*perfect*", and has a divine sense ('the Language of God'). In his treatise the "Astadahyayi" (eight books), Panini set a formal approach based on rules and definitions to describe the Sanskrit, comparing its sacred text and the usual language of communication. This was achieved with the goal of preserving the Hindu religious texts; i.e.: "The Vedic hymns". Panini produced a comprehensive and scientific theory concerning morphology, phonetics, and phonology.

His grammar consists of ordered (mathematical) rules. He was also the initiator of the use of letters of the alphabet to represent numbers. The Indian way of representing numbers by words is originated from his systemization of Sanskrit grammar, and hence, mathematics becoming an outcome of the development of linguistics in India. English critic, Joseph Carpenter, said that: "An indirect consequence of Panini's efforts to increase the linguistic facility of Sanskrit became apparent in the character of scientific and mathematical literature."

Panini's work on Sanskrit was far more elaborate, accurate, systematic, and exhaustive than any similar Western grammar of the nineteenth century. He dealt with grammar by a "Sutra style", meaning string and thread. Sutra means "holy style", consisting of few letters containing clarity, essence and open on all sides without ambiguity. It is characterized by economy of expression, using a number of devices which are brief and precise called "Anuverti & Adhikaas". His grammar was derivational; its main concern was to derive grammatically correct sentences and phrases. He succeeded in providing a complete syntactic, morphological and phonological description of Sanskrit.

He did not view words in isolation, but as units belonging to a syntactic structure. He viewed language as a whole and integrated system. The sentence is the basis of the derivational process. In addition to this, he was also concerned with accentuation and punctuation.

The semantic side in Panini's grammatical analysis was left relatively unattended. He almost neglected this side of linguistic analysis; claiming that meaning is not part of the linguistic subject; similar to Bloomfield's position: "It can be learned through the worldly usages". For Panini, grammar is a science that studies the use of correct words and sentences. In fact, he used semantics in order to keep the formal considerations of language. For instance, he gave rules to derive the verbal and nominal forms through affixation, which is part of semantic categories.

He did use aspects of semantics in his grammar in a few ways (concepts). First, the concept of "Vertamaan" (present time), "Bahuta" (plurality), and stating rules that replace the corresponding phonological form.

He also used semantic concepts that are necessary to organize words into groups or classes "Verna" (meaning color). The shades of meaning were conveyed by the derived words consisting of the root and the suffixes or compounds.

Panini's grammar aimed at providing a systematic grammar of Sanskrit. It is the foundation of all subsequent grammars of Sanskrit. It is synchronic and comparative in the sense that it deals with the difference between the spoken language and the Vedic sacred language.

It consists of:

1) 4000 grammatical rules

2) Identification of philological segments

3) 2000 verbal roots

4) Inventory of idiosyncrasies.

As a final word, Panini's grammar keeps with the Indian traditions in life such as 'sutras' (holy style), rituals and yoga, which are analyzable by an explicit rule system. Panini's "Astadhyayi" is not philosophical in nature, but purely aimed at linguistic description. Still, his Sutras remained the guide for all the philosophers and grammarians in India, and are still much quoted for various kinds of linguistic theories and philosophical concepts.

ARISTOTLE (384-322 BC)

Aristotle was 'the absolute intellectual,' in the sense that he touched on every field of knowledge without distinction. He was first of all a philosopher and a logician, but like so many other intellectuals had soon noticed that language was the key to all knowledge, and that the limit of words means the limits of knowledge!

Aristotle was the tutor of Alexander the Great. He was born in Macedonia. Together with Plato, he is considered as one of the greatest philosophers that the world has ever known. He was a true scholar and academic with an interest in several intellectual disciplines ranging from astronomy and rhetoric to politics and philosophy. His major was certainly logic. Aristotelian logic, also known as *Formal Logic* is based on PROPOSITION, SYLLOGISM and CONTRADICTION. He set the rules of formal logic in his notorious book *The Organon*.

1. Truth

Truth has been the main concern of logicians, philosophers and semioticians, in the past and the present. They divide truth into analytic (deductive) and synthetic (observational). In the absence of the latter they use the former. In the beginning, there is the word. Each word is connected to concepts, and then comes syntax into play. The combination of two words or more opens the door for truth. It is technically known as sentence or proposition. A proposition can be either true (T) or false (F). Each discourse consists of premises (propositions) and a conclusion (a proposition). If the premises are true the conclusion is true and if the premises are false the conclusion is false. Meaning can also shift from denotation which is (original sense) to connotation which is open-ended, for example the use (and misuse) of words like *popular, freedom, democracy*, etc.

Proposition consists of a subject followed by a predicate. The subject is usually an entity; e.g. a person, an object:

The teacher is here.

The chair is here.

The predicate is an attribute of the subject. According to Aristotle, the number of predicates is 10, referred to as the 10 categories:

2. The Ten Categories

Substance (man, horse)

Quantity (two cm long)

Quality (white, grammatical)

Relation (double, half, greater)

Place (in the lyceum, last year)

Position (lies, sits)

State (has shoes)

Action (cuts, burns)

Affection (is cut, is burnt)

(*Arabic & Logical Form*, p. 92)

3. Proposition

We will be mainly concerned with analytic truth value of propositions. The truth value of each proposition is fixed by a binary system consisting of either a tautology (T) or a contradiction (F). Consider the following proposition:

It is cold and windy.

This proposition can be analyzed as consisting of two logically equivalent propositions:

It is cold, and

It is windy.

The first one can be either true or false. If we posit that it is true then its negation must be false and vice versa: if we posit that it is false then its negation must be true. Call it P and its negation –P; we can obtain the following truth-table:

P   -P

T   F

F   T

The friend of my friend is my friend,

The enemy of my friend is my enemy

The friend of my enemy is my enemy

The enemy of my enemy is my friend!

Considering the compound proposition (conjunction): 'it is cold and windy' that we have analyzed as consisting of two propositions; call them P and Q; its truth-table will be as follows:

P	Q	P&Q
T	T	T
T	F	F
F	T	F
F	F	F

(*Generative Grammar*, p.55)

4. Contradiction

A contradiction is the combination of two propositions sharing the same subject and the same categories; except that one is affirmative and the other negative. The truth value of a contradiction is always false (F).

P	-P	P&-P
T	F	F
F	T	F

Dialectics is based on contradiction.

5. Syllogism

A syllogism consists of a major premise, a minor premise and a conclusion, e.g.

All men must die. (MAJOR PREMISE)

Socrates is a man. (MINOR PREMISE)

Socrates must die. (CONCLUSION)

To reach the conclusion, you play down the middle term, in our case men/man (i.e. the subject of the major premise and the predicate of the minor premise) and you join the subject of the minor premise with the predicate of the major premise.

Moving to metaphysical considerations, Aristotle again used syllogism to state: "since motion must always exist and must not cease, there must necessarily be something, either one thing or many, that first initiated motion, and this first mover must be unmoved –the unmoved mover: GOD [THEOS]."

(*Arabic & Logical Form*, p. 93)

6. Conditionals

Conditional proposition is a compound of two propositions; the truth of one depends on the truth of the other (disjunction vs. implication). It is a stipulation, or provision, that needs to be satisfied; also, something that must exist or be the case or happen in order for something else to do so (as in 'the will to live is a condition for survival').

Conditional proposition is a sentence/proposition of the form 'If A then B':

A disjunction is true if one part is true and the other false:

You are either a Moroccan or a non-Moroccan.

You are either Moroccan or French.

A conditional proposition (implication) is true if both parts are true and false if both parts are false as in:

If I had money I would be happy.

Conditionals are either hypothetical or categorial (see Encyclopedia Britannica, vol. 3, p. 521)

If all the seas were one sea what a great sea that would be,

If all the men were one man what a great man that would be,

If all the trees were one tree what a great tree that would be,

If all the axes were one axe what a great axe that would be.

And if the great man took the great axe,

Cut down the great tree and,

Let it fall into the great sea,

What a splish-splash that would be!

HEBREW TRADITION

Hebrew tradition has an exceptional longevity ever since Moses (14th c BC). It includes the Jewish history, theology and language.

1. History

1.1. Prophet Moses

Moses saw the fire and spoke to God face-to-face. He delivered his people from Egyptian slavery. By the Covenant on Mount Sinai, where he received the Ten Commandments, he founded the nation of Israel. He is revered as a great Prophet and teacher in Judaism, Christianism and Islam. His influence is also tremendous in the Western culture and civilization in general.

When he saw the burning bush on the Holy Mountain of Sinai, the LORD called him by his name and asked him to 'take off your sandals!' He bowed down to the ground. He was ordered to go to the Pharaoh and ask him: 'Let my people go!' They must leave Egypt to a land of Milk and Honey! God's Name was revealed to him as: 'I AM WHO I AM!' (Exodus 3:14).

Moses suffered at the Jewish mobs several times. They complained, protested and took rocks to stone him on several occasions. Before his death, He promised them a 'prophet from among their brethren.' (Deuteronomy 18:18)

1.2. Philosopher Maimonides

Maimonides was the most important Jewish philosopher. His name was Moses Ibn Maimon (referred to as Maimonides). He lived in Andalusia (Islamic Spain) in the 12th c. His works include philosophy, theology, and medicine. He was a student of renowned Muslim philosopher, jurist and physician Averroes (Ibn Rushd). Some consider him, wrongly, as 'his Xerox copy!'

His writings were composed in Arabic and Hebrew. He dealt with Jewish law, logic and metaphysics. His most influential work *Guide for the Perplexed* was written in Arabic. It took him 15 years to achieve. It assumed a Gestalt approach, i.e. once the general is understood, the details will be grasped without problem. He further influenced later philosophers such as Spinoza and Leibniz. Still, his ideas aroused much opposition from Jews themselves.

Some of his propositions are not without reminding us of Wittgenstein's "fly metaphor."

Listen to this: 'Some of them (people) have turned their backs to the King's House; looking in the opposite direction. Others are heading towards the king's house with the intention of entering and bowing to him in respect, but still haven't seen the walls of the King's house. Some have reached the house but are turning round, trying to find the door. Some have entered the door, and are wandering in the caves of the house. Some have reached the main room of the house and are with the King in the same room, but still cannot see the King or speak to him. They need another wandering so as to see the King and listen to him and talk to him.' (Maimonides, 714, 149 'King's House' and 'gentiles')

So far so good! But listen to this: 'I am explaining to you this parable, that I have created to say: those who are outside the city are every individual without religion or any traditional idea e.g. those Turks of the Far North, and also those Sudanese of the Far South, and likewise those living with us in these regions. Those are like unspeaking animals... monkeys (?)' (*Perplexed*, p. 714)

The Jews are perplexed indeed, concerning their status (favoured) amongst the nations. (The Koran 2:47) They are, more importantly, perplexed concerning the Name of God. As a philosopher, Maimonides was supposed to clear all their confusions. He did not.

He also proved to be a poor linguist when he dealt with the Name of God: 'All His Mighty Names, which are found in books, are derived from verbs, except one which is YHWH (=Yahweh). This is the accidental Name of His Majesty. This is why it is called the Supreme Devine Name.' (ibid, p. 149)

Maimonides is no exception to Wittgenstein's proposition: 'philosophers don't help the fly get out of the bottle. Rather, they lure it in!' The Name of God is mentioned more than 19 times in the very first page of the Hebrew Torah alone as ELOH! How couldn't the greatest Jewish philosopher see it? (cf. Deedat)

2. Theology

Jewish theology is based on the trilogy Y-H-V-H (Tetragrammaton for God), the Chosen people of God and their Promised Land.

According to Saussure (and the linguists in general), there is a staunch relationship between names and entities (concepts). The existence of a Supreme Being is shared by all nations. Different cultures have given Him different names though. The Japanese call him Kami, the Hindus Rama, the Christians Jesus, the Muslims Allah. The Name of God is a problem in Judaism!

The Jews boast of being the exceptional detainees of monotheism and the true Name of God (the one that opened the sea for Moses!) No one has the right to utter it expect the highest rabbis (Y-H-V-H). They hide it by surnames such as Adonai, Hashem, etc. Still the first reader of the first page of the Torah will find the name of God plain as ELOH-IM, the same name, shortened came when Jacob supposedly wrestled with Him, and hence the name Isra-el and Beth-el. The same applies to Jesus final cry: ELAI! (cf. Matthew 27:46).

3. Language

Hebrew, a Sacred Language.

'The transformation of Hebrew into a sacred language is, of course, bound up with the political fate of the people. In the period following the return from the Babylonian Exile, Aramaic, a cognate of Hebrew, functioned as the international or imperial language in official life and certainly gained a foothold as a vernacular. It did not, despite claims made by some scholars, displace the everyday Hebrew of the people. The language of the Mishna, far from being a scholar's dialect, seems to reflect – in the same way as the Koine (common) Greek of the New Testament – popular speech. Displacement of Hebrew – both in its literary form in Scriptures and in its popular usage – did take place in the Diaspora, however, as evidenced by the need to translate Scriptures into Greek in some communities and into Aramaic in others. As far as the emerging order of worship is concerned, there seems also to have been an inclination on the part of some authorities to permit even the recitation of the Shema complex in the vernacular. Struggles over these issues within the communities continued for a number of centuries in various places, but the development of formal literary Hebrew – a sacred tongue, to be used side by side with the Hebrew Scriptures in worship – brought them to an end. Although the communities of the Diaspora used the vernaculars of their environment in day-to-day living and even – as in the case of the communities of the Islamic world – for philosophical, theological, and other scholarly writings, in worship, Hebrew remained the standard until modern times when some of the reform movements in western Europe sought partially – and a very small fraction even totally – to displace it.' (Encyclopaedia Britannica)

3.1. Holy Book

The Torah is the Holy Book of the Jews. It has many versions, one of which is the Septuagint, 'the first translation of the old testament into Greek, the Septuagint (translated by 70 scholars). 'Hebrew linguistic scholarship was developed under the influence of Arabic linguistic work. This was due both to the structural similarities of these two Semitic languages and to the political power of the Arabs after the Islamic expansion over the near east, North Africa, and Spain. Technical terms and categories were borrowed from Arabic linguists for the descriptive analysis of Hebrew.' (Robins, p. 16, 97)

Its spelling and pronunciation pose certain problems to the Jewish scholars. 'Certain aspects of the data presented here are rather controversial. As with any language that is no longer living, biblical Hebrew is subject to conflicting interpretations of the orthographic record. On another level, the fact that no aspect of the orthography other than the consonants demonstrably dates earlier than the 6th c. AD has led some scholars to conclude that certain aspects of the traditional pronunciation were borrowed from the native language of post-biblical speakers of Hebrew. On the other hand, we know that a long oral tradition of study and memorization preceded the fixing of the non-consonantal orthography. The parallel to the reputed accuracy of transcription of Vedic Sanskrit is not inappropriate here. The, to my mind, correct view of this matter is embodied in the statement of Orlinsky (1966) that the Masoretes, the medieval scholars, "from first to last were essentially preservers and recorders of the pronunciation of Hebrew as they heard it." (McCarthy, p. 35)

3.2. Sound System

Following Spinoza's hypotheses 'the grammarians have rightly divided the letters into five classes: guttural, labial, dental, lingual, palatal, which are respectively:

Guttural: alef, h, H , ʕ-

Labial: b, w, m, x

Palatal: g, y, k, q

Lingual: d, s, l, n, t

Dental: z, s, ts, r, sh' (Spinoza, pp. 39, 67) (*harf* (letter) in Arabic means: lateral, side, turned from its original form).

3.3. Hebrew Vowels

There are 10 vowels in Hebrew: 5 short and five long ones.

Short vowels

Patah /a/ [IPA value]

Segol /e/

Hiriq /i/

Qubuts /u/

X /?/ [schwa?]

Long vowels

Qamats /a:/

Tsere /e:/

Hiriq gadol /i:/

Shuruq /u:/

Holam /o:/

3.4. Nouns

Grammatically, Spinoza considers the noun as the most important lexical category: 'concerning nouns, it must be stressed that through substantive proper noun we can express only one singular individual. Every individual has only one single noun and so for each action. So each substantive as well as infinitive and adverb i.e. adjectives of actions to which they must agree in number are expressed in singular. The other nouns are expressed in singular and in plural as well.'

The phonetic system of Hebrew is similar to that of Arabic. Sibawaihi has set out systematically the organs of speech and the mechanism of utterance, interpreting articulations as the interference with egressive (i.e. outward airstream) in various ways by different configurations of the vocal tract. The modes of interference were designated *maxraj*, literally 'outlet' by which the air made its exit. (Robins, p. 98)

3.5. Phonological Transformations

In phonology there are several processes (transformations), such as spirantization, word-boundary, etc.

'Hebrew *ganvu* 'they stole' from underlying g-n-B, but the context of spirantization has gone after reduction applies; the underlying form might even all but disappear in the output, as in *hitu* 'they extended', in which only the /t/ remains from the underlying root /ntC/ (C a "weak" consonant).' (Chomsky 1995, p. 224)

3.6. Non-Concatenative Morphology

Hebrew morphology is similar to Arabic morphology. We may borrow the work of famous Arabic grammarians here. Sibawaihi recognized three word classes, inflected nouns and verbs and uninflected particle. The description of verbal inflections was mostly based on 'triliteral' roots, familiar in such examples as *k-t-b*, write, hence come *kataba*, he wrote, *kitaab*, book, etc.

3.7. Concatenation

It is a term used in formal representation of linguistic structures, especially in generative grammar, to refer to a process for forming strings of elements, the elements being seen in a relation of linear succession, e.g. X+Y+Z i.e. they are chained together. (Crystal, 1985, p. 78) Arabic and Hebrew are non-concatenative.

3.8. Syntactic Transformations

According to Noam Chomsky, it is possible in syntax, as in morphology (g-n-B → *ganvu* 'they stole') to formulate the desired result in terms of input-output:

תודה לאל! הצפון והדרום, אתה יצרת אותם

The North and the South, YOU created them. (Psalms 89:13)

ARABIC TRADITION (I): SIBAWAIHI

'Whoever wants to write about grammar after Sibawaihi let him feel humble!' (Mazini)

'About 50 years ago, I studied Sibawaihi's grammar in an advanced Arabic course and was much intrigued.' (Chomsky)

1. Introduction

This is the first grammar of Arabic. It is religiously motivated as far as content is concerned. It was devised to describe the language of the Holy Qur'an. Its form is most poetic trying to 'marry the beautiful to the useful.' This is seen in the use of terms such as *bab* 'Gate (of the Castle of Grammar)' rather than chapter, *shams* 'sun' feature rather than coronal, *ſilah* letters for glides (semi vowels), etc.

Al-Kitab has earned much applause world-wide to the extent that French André Roman (Université de Lyon II) used to say: 'We must stand up by respect when recalling what Sibawaihi and Khalil have left us in phonetics alone!' Sibawaihi's name itself is poetic viz. 'apple-smell'. His book is known as *Al-Kitab* i.e. 'The Book!'

In the preliminaries of his book, Sibawaihi determines the categories of Arabic as a trilogy: N, V and P only. He defines what is *Hasan* good (acceptable) and what is *qabiH* 'bad' such as

'I drank the sea, I carried the mountain, I came tomorrow and will come yesterday'. Soon he tackles to the essential keys of Arabic grammar (and would influence all Arabic grammar after him viz. transformation and government). There is a gate of the V that transits to zero, one, two, etc. objects.

Other gates concern the transitivity of verbs and transformation viz. the gate of essence and accident e.g. *Ya Allah!* (O! God!)

2. Sound System

2.1. Sound Outlets

Sibawaihi divides the speech tract into four sections which are pharynx, tongue, lips and nasal cavity. Each of which is then divided into far, middle and front. The pharynx produces 6 sounds /*alif*, ʔ, ʕ, H, h, R/. The tongue produces (active articulator) many sounds. The lips produce /b, m, w/ the nasal cavity (light) n. the vowels seem to be absent [?]. Then he moves to the distinctive features.

2.2. Distinctive Features

Sibawaihi defines a set of (binary) distinctive features such as voice, stop, lateral, nasal, roll, vowel, velarized, etc. voiceless sounds are gathered in fa *Hatthahu shaXSun sakat* 'someone urged him so he kept silent'. Coronal is called *shams* 'sun letters' by opposition to moon (-coronal).

2.3. Phonological Processes

Sibawaihi deals with phonetic transformations such as assimilation as in the article *ʔal-* with its neighboring sound, whether it is +coronal or –coronal. He deals with the behavior of feminine /t/ and /k/ sounds in end-boundary as in *qa:lat Fatimah* 'Fatima said' *shbish*? 'whassup?' It can be deleted in the noun (turned into /h/) but is kept in verb. (clitic)(feminine)

Assimilation of labio-nasal *nb* into *mb* in *ʔamber* 'amber' is a case of regressive assimilation. Most assimilations are regressive *ash-shams* 'the sun'. Progressive assimilation is found in examples such as *ʔimdaHHilalan* 'praise crescent'. Loan words such as *pirind* (sword) (Farsi) are spirantized (Chomsky & Crystal) since Arabic lacks p/v it becomes *firind*.

The canonical syllable structure in Arabic is CV. Some instances that seem to disturb this are remedied by the insertion of a vowel as in *aHadun+ALLAH* 'one Allah' nl → nil. The reverse happens. Too many CV syllables in succession is not light (one of the theories of Arabic sound system) as in *yaDaraba* 'he is hitting' restructured into *yaDribu* CVCCVCV.

3. Non-Concatenative Morphology

Noun is considered as the origin '*asl*' of lexical items *fiʕl* (verb). Verbs are said to be derived from noun (as they are tense less, simple, kernel). The noun can undergo morphological transformations i.e. deletion (final truncation), substitution, etc. as in O! Allah!

Both noun and verb in Arabic are based on a trilateral root C-C-C which (Robins) denotes a general meaning, which is then converted into different words [] by the insertion of melodies and then transformations may operate such as imperfective, causative *nazzala* 'bring down', sick, etc. the most 'popular' transformation in textbooks of Arabic grammar is imperfective. It follows the lines of at least three analogies which can be found in examples such as *qatala* 'kill' *Daraba* 'hit' *Hasiba* 'think'. Their respective patterns are:

'he did'	'he will do':
faʕila	yafʕulu
faʕala	yafʕilu
faʕila	yafʕalu

The central vowel seems to play a crucial role in determining the pattern of the imperfective verb. These analogies are extremely productive.

Sick verb (including glides) are turned from one to the other (for lightness sake) *waʕada* 'he promised'. Bare verb/basic can be 'clothed' as it were increased by the addition of one or more redundancy (Ibn Malik, cf. *Three Good Traditions*) letter found in the sentence *saʔaltumu:ni:ha:* 'you asked for her' e.g. *ʔadkhala* 'make enter' also realized (causative) by a doubling of central consonant *dakhkhala* 'ask enter.'

4. Transformational Syntax

Arabic is supposedly V.S.O. language. In fact its syntax is much more elaborate as it allows more than one word-order VSO, SVO, VOS, etc. It also displays a double sentence structure (cop-drop), i.e. nominal and verbal sentences.

As far as nominal sentence structure is concerned, it is found by a subject directly followed by a predicate (cop-drop). Carter believes that I.C.A. can apply to it. It's quite hazy *hatha ʔaXu:ka* 'this (is) your brother.'

Case plays a crucial role in determining word-order as well as thematic relations in a sentence as in *man Daraba ʔaXu:ka* (whom did your brother hit?). Nominative is marked by u while accusative is marked by a as in *man Daraba ʔaXa:ka* 'who hit your brother?' (Triton & Comrie). It turns from agent to patient with an inversion of theta roles.

Sibawaihi first considers the canonical nominal sentence structure which consists of subject plus predicate []. In fact Arabic displays two major sentence (minor sentence) structures viz. nominal and verbal (with interchange).

The sentence can have two readings depending on the case of the object. It could either question *man Daraba ʔa**Xa**:ka* 'who hit your brother' or *man Daraba ʔa**Xu**:ka* 'whom did your brother hit?' with who agent . Case determines the whole LF of the sentence (cf. Chomsky??) With who agent by case ending of *ʔa**Xu**:ka* 'your brother.' **u** nominative agent and **a** accusative patient.

Transformation (movement) are used for focus (as the major theme of the proposition) as in *ʔijja:ka naʕbudu* 'Thee alone we worship' in which worship is excluded except for one viz. God.

Transformations are considered a necessary tool of interpretation of sentences. Since sentence *ʔisʔali Lqaryata* 'you ask the village' breaks selectional restrictions. You do not ask a village since village is (-human). Sibawaihi postulates the existence of a deep structure of the form *ʔisʔali ʔahla lqaryati* 'ask the people of the village,' and then a deletion transformation which yields the above sentence. Likewise for the verse *makru llayli wa nnahar* 'the plotting of day and night.' In some sentences, Sibawaihi noted an alternation of case (passivization of intransitives). Either the first NP is nominative and the last accusative or vice versa. Both are acceptable *si:ra* 'travelled' (cf. Chomsky 1981).

Besides transformation, Government is another key notion in Arabic grammar. Arabic grammarians have dealt with it extensively. They have established a government hierarchy, conflict and power. Government usually requires sisterhood plus adjacency?

It determines case and theta relations. Each category has its own government properties. As far as hierarchy is concerned the verb is considered as the top governor since it can govern a large number of arguments/NPs. It can assign [] two Cases [], it can allow movement of its own objects and even deletion without losing its governing power. This is illustrated respectively in in *ʔiyya:ka naʕbudu* 'Thee alone we worship' and *kilayhima wa tamran* 'both plus dates.'

Conflict in government occurs when two governors dispute the same governee, one trying to assign nominative and one accusative to it. Ultimately the closest (adjacent) as *Darabtu wa Darabani Zaid* 'I hit and was hit by Zaid' *ʔinna Allah* 'lo! Allah…'

Inflection richness allows the shift SVO/VSO as in *qa:la qawmuka/qawmuka qa:lu:* 'your people said/said your people' as noted in Chomsky's Minimalist Program.

ARABIC TRADITION (II): IBN JINNI

1. Arabic

Arabic is a Semitic language together with Hebrew and Aramaic (Wright, 1979). At the present time, it is the Lingua Franca of the Arab World (Muslim World?). The word 'Arab' like the word 'Hebrew' were used originally to describe "passers-by" i.e. nomads traveling in search of better lands for their cattle in the desert. Now-a-days the Arab world stretches from Morocco in the west to Iraq in the east, where it is the state language. The Arabic language is a state of Diglossia, i.e. a high Arabic and a number of national dialects. Other classifications could include Literary Arabic, Classical Arabic, Modern Standard Arabic usually referred to as *al-fuSHa* ('the purest Arabic').

2. Arabic and Islam

Classical Arabic (CA) is the language of ancient Arabic poetry (The 7 Poems). Starting from the 6th c., it has become primarily the language of the Holy Koran (Marmaduke Pickthall). It is the language of Islam *par excellence*. Most of the world's Muslims do not speak Arabic as their native language, but many can read the Koranic script and recite the Koran. Among non-Arab Muslims, translations of the Koran are accompanied by the original Arabic text. At the present time, yet another form of (High) Arabic is recognized. It is called Modern Standard Arabic (MSA).

3. The Structure of Arabic

As can be found, with more or less accuracy, in the other Semitic languages (Hebrew and Aramaic), Arabic has a special verb morphology. It consists of a set of non-concatenative techniques for the building of words from roots (Robins 1967). The root consists of discontinuous stretch of, usually three consonants to which a discontinuous a set of (usually two) vowels is inserted to obtain words. For instance the root *k-t-b* which carries a general (vague) idea of writing. It needs the insertion of the discontinuous vowel pattern *a-a* to yield the words: *kataba* 'he wrote' *katabat* 'she wrote' *katabta* 'you wrote'. (Palmer 1985) (Ibn Malik '*bi faʕlala...*'). Many patterns are possible (see Ibn Jinni's Derivational transformations). Usually the addition of pronominal clitic pronouns at the end completes the so-called Arabic one-word-sentence as in: *ʔakal-tu* 'I ate'.

4. Life

Ibn Jinni was born in 932 in Mosul (Iraq), the son of a Greco-Roman slave belonging to Sulaiman bnu Ahmad al-Azdi. He had several teachers, the most notorious of which was Abu Ali al-Farisi, the leader of Basra School and most famous linguist of the time. Ibn Jinni entered his circle from the age of fifteen and followed him in his numerous travels. He was keen on recording his teacher's comments, observations and remarks besides collecting data from the Bedouins (*Wabar*). They were both present at several royal courts, such as the court of *Sayf ad-Dawla* (945-967) in Aleppo and the court of ADud ad-*Dawla* (949-983) in *Faris*. According to the historian Yaqut, Ibn Jinni took an office at the court of *ADud ad-Dawla* and *Shamsu ad-Dawla* (983-987), where he met and made excellent friends with famous poet al-Mutanabi (915-965). He became the interpreter of Mutanabi's poetic Divans, *par excellence*. They held each other in extremely high esteem, to the extent that the poet entrusted the grammarian with free interpretation of his Divans and said about him: 'that is a man whose value is unknown to many.' Ibn Jinni took over the leadership of Arabic scholarship after Abu Ali's death, until he himself passed away in 1002.

5. Books

Ibn Jinni's major works are *al-Khasa'is*, and *sir sinaat l-irab*... He left some 50 books dedicated to the 'Arabic noble language', as he called it. He mainly dealt with the phonetics, phonology and morphology of Arabic. In his book *sir sinaat l-irab* (the secret of parsing!!!) he describes the vowels and consonants of Arabic, their characteristics, classification, the nature of the segments (strong and weak), assimilation, metathesis, substitution and other phonetic transformations. His book *tasrif l-muluk* (Kings' Morphological Transformations) is a treaties of detailed derivation processes in which he analyses the (simple and complex) morphological forms. In *al-Khasa'is* he deals with the grammatical principles, based on his study of the language of the Bedouins of Mosul (Iraq). It is his biggest book, which consists of some 162 chapters that summarize his enormous Arabic linguistic knowledge. He is also the author of numerous commentaries on the works of Ali Al-Farisi, a commentary on Mazini's *tasrif* (Mazini's Morphology). He wrote commentaries on Mutabi's poetic divans. Besides being a master of Arabic phonetics, morphology, syntax and semantics, he was also a literary man and a poet.

6. Theories

The most important theories of Ibn Jinni are transformation, derivation, analogy, argument, etc. As an example of syntactic transformation, he gives the example of the Koranic verse: "And ask the village", which has the input (and meaning): "ask (the people) of the village." A deletion transformation has taken place. Generally speaking, transformations can also apply by addition or compensation, etc. (cf. Sibawaihi). As far as *ishtiqaq* 'morphological derivation' is concerned, Ibn Jinni distinguishes two types: Minor and Major derivations. As an example of minor derivation, from the root *s-l-m*, you can derive *silm* 'peace', *salam* 'security', etc. (Robins). Major derivation may start from a root such as *k-l-m*, to derive the words such as: *kallama* 'to hit', *malaka* 'to possess', etc.

As for the connection between "expression-meaning" Ibn Jinni believes in a strong, almost natural relationship between the two sides of the "linguistic coin." To support his theory, he gives examples of verbs describing the sounds made by the wind, the birds, the acts of eating, etc., in which the sounds seem to mirror the actions.

Although Ibn Jinni's contribution in the field of Arabic philology is enormous; in fact, he devoted himself mainly to the study of grammar, proving a major interest in lexicon and morphology without forgetting semantics and pragmatics.

Ibn Jinni is seen as the highest authority in the field of linguistic discipline *taSrif* (morphological derivation). He is also considered as the founder of the science of *al-ishtiqāq al-akbar* (etymology). As a philologist, he has occupied a middle position between the two famous schools of Arabic linguistics of his time Kufa and BaSra. He eventually took the side of the Baghdadi school (*samaʕ* 'attested data' and *qiyas* 'analogy').

7. Semantics

Ibn Jinni's work is usually associated with Arabic phonology and morphology. In fact, Ibn Jinni must also be associated with semantics, especially in his theory of *taSaqub* ('onomatopoeia').

The Arabic language is one of the many languages that have been the focus of extensive semantic studies. In fact, the study of Arabic has contributed much to semantics. It all stemmed from the huge work devoted to *tafsir* 'the interpretation of the Holy Koran'.

Some also attribute much semantic work to Ibn Jinni's works as can be found in his books *al-muhtasab, al-khasais, al-munsif* in which he discusses certain social semantics problems i.e. 'pragmatics' to use the modern terminology as opposed to grammatical semantics.

Ibn Jinni was not just a philologist of Arabic; he was a philosopher of language.

BERBER TRADITION

'awid aman! awid aRtum!'

"The Berber languages are widely scattered over North Africa and the Sahara. In many places they have been supplanted by Arabic, but are still used as the home languages in many areas. *Kabyle*, *Shilh*, *Zenaga*, and *Tuareg* are among the best known." (Gleason 1968)

1. Introduction

The first thing that comes to mind when we speak about Berbers is their dance. Their tattooed women dancing and singing in 'unintelligible' words, in strange tunes in the Atlas Mountains! Then we learn that the Berbers of Morocco, (...) are divided into northern (Rif), middle (Atlas Mountains) and south (Sus). As a matter of fact, Morocco has got two native languages; one sacred (Arabic) spoken mainly in the cities, and one (3 dialects) spoken in the mountains (Berber). The search in the origin of the people (and their languages) takes one to three different directions at least: the dictionaries define them as 'a Caucasian Muslim race.' Some say they came from Yemen (or Germany?). Some claim that they were all the time 'Here' in North Africa (?)

Later on, as a linguist I noticed the universal trilogy 'language-race-culture.' And following Kenneth Pike (1982) I believe that "the problem challenging translators (language researchers) laid both beyond (words) in the sentence, and beyond the sentence in discourse and beyond discourse itself in the socio-cultural framework in which the target language is spoken." Language is linked to culture, and culture necessarily means history. So studying the history of Morocco is crucial to understand its linguistic problems.

2. History

We can try to study the history of Morocco starting from the immemorial time of its original inhabitants. Still, the question of 'original inhabitants' is always a controversial and often an ideological question. Generally speaking, it is agreed that the early inhabitants of Morocco are the Berbers. They were a nomad people.

The history of Morocco (North Africa at large) is actually a long stretch of time starting from prehistory. It becomes more accessible, starting from the arrival of the Phoenicians (and their 'Berber' script). They came from present day Lebanon to North Africa. They wanted to have a foot on each side of the Mediterranean. They built mighty Cartage, which was destined to meet another mighty power - that of Rome. (see The Punic Wars)

In the 7th c. came the Arabs with their language and the religion of Islam, to which the Berbers soon converted. The conquest of Spain was actually achieved by Berber leader Tariq Ibn Ziyad (hence the appellation 'Gibraltar'). Then in 1492, the Muslims and the Jews were violently chased from Catholic

Spain. Many among them made Morocco their new home and brought in the culture of Andalusia.

Starting from the 16th c. European powers started establishing colonies on the coasts of Morocco. Many wars followed, the most famous of which was that of the 'Battle of the Three Kings (all lost their lives), in 1578. Then Morocco knew a period of isolation until the French colonization of Algeria. In 1844, the Moroccan army tried to help the Algerians against the French but was dramatically defeated for lack of weapons (I suppose) at Isly river (Oujda). The French language became mandatory. Spain took the North (Rif). The Spanish language came in and is still much used in the north of Morocco besides Berber.

In 1904, England exchanged its sphere of dominance with France; it was Morocco for Egypt. The two superpowers agreed France took Morocco and England Egypt. In 1912, Morocco became a French protectorate (protected from the Germans?). The painful protectorate lasted from 1912 to 1956. Morocco was under the command of General Lyautey.

World War II saw the arrival of a third super power – the Americans. The 'Old Blood-and-Guts' General Patton arrived from the west coast (Casablanca) and crushed the French resistance. The French lost one thousand soldiers, the Americans two hundred. English came in powerfully.

Each one of the above mentioned invaders brought in his language. The last to come always has the higher 'prestige,' as the Arabic saying goes: 'the defeated takes the habits (including the language) of the winner!' So it was Berber, Arabic, French and Spanish, and finally English. Nowadays, 'all Moroccans' want to speak (American) English.

3. Language

The Berber Language(s) "Tamazight" belongs to the Hamito-Semitic language family. It is spoken in North Africa as well as in parts of Mali, Niger, and the Canary islands. Some linguists claim that there are 30 Berber dialects at least, with the Touareg (les 'Hommes Bleux') who have kept the 'purest Tamazight.' It is written from left to right in the *Tafinagh* script (ancient Phoenician). It is spoken by some 30 million people. In 2003, the king of Morocco decreed Berber as the third official language of the country besides Arabic and French. It is to be used in administrations, the mass media and has departments in every Moroccan University. The southern dialect (Susi) seems to have set itself as 'standard' amongst conflicting and rival Berber dialects. This is probably by the force of some of its influence, at the expense of the others.

3.1. Verb Morphology in Tarifit

Verbs in Tarifit (…) can express different ideas and actions; there are dynamic and static ones. There are transitive, intransitive (…) for instance:

/ksi-x-t/ (took it)

/ksi/ (to take)

/x/ (I)

/t/ (it/him/her)

(Mounach Mostafa)

3.2. Ouhalla's Syntactic Theories

As far as Berber's syntactic structure is concerned; it has (), many similarities with Arabic (and other Semitic languages). VSO, Pro Drop, Cop Drop, etc. are among its syntactic features:

Isha Faris aGrum

eat Faris bread

'Faris eats bread'

Isha-th Faris

eat-it Faris

'Faris eats it'

Isha-th/ishi th (Mounach)

( ) eats-it

'He eats it'

Faris argaz

Faris () a man

'Faris is a man'

Among other things, Ouhalla (1988) deals with the structure of nominal and prepositional, and head-movement process involved in their derivation in Berber and other languages () nouns in Berber are marked morphologically for the number and gender features.

a- ḥamosh

"boy"

b- taḥamosh-t

"girl"

c- *i ḥamosh-(i)n*

"children"

He further, compares Berber clitic syntax with its equivalents in French and Italian:

- *Jean les a lues*

- *Gianni li vuole vedere*

   'Ginni wants to see them'

-*Ad-t   ja-rzam/tawwart*

Will-it 3sm-open/door

'He will open the door'

The objective clitic pronoun *les* moves to the (pre) auxiliary position, leaving the agreement marker *–es* attached to the verb *lu*. In Italian, the operation is more interesting as it takes the objective clitic *li* from the embedded clause to the matrix clause. Berber is also classified as a 'null subject language.'

Jussad

Came (he)

'he came'

Movement transformations are responsible for moving words/phrase from an original (deep) structure to a surface structure. The same thing applies to clitic (affixed pronouns), which move and attach to the nearest word in Arabic and Berber:

- *Daraba-hu Ali*

Hit-3sm-him Ali

'Ali hit him'

- *Kitaabu-hu*

Book-his

'His book'

- *La-hu*

'To him'

A movement transformation can take zero, one or two steps in different languages. In English it stands for naught:

John opened it with the key.

No movement.

In Arabic the pronoun moves one step:

[*Fataha-haa*] Ali

Opened-it Ali

'Ali opened it.'

In Berber and Italian two steps:

a. *[[ʔa-t-irzaam] Ali] ss-saruut*

'Will-it-open-3sm Ali with-key'

'Ali will open it with the key.'

b. *[[Gianni **li**] vuole] vedere*

'Gianni wants to see them.'

3.3. Susi Idioms

John Lyons (1968) considers idioms as "incomplete sentences generated by the grammar but differ from them in that their description does not involve the application of the rules established to account for the vast mass of mere normal sentences.

These are what de Saussure has called 'readymade utterances' (*locutions toutes faites*)

In Susi:

ma jussan uRju:l izkanʒbi:r

'What does the donkey know about ginger?'

Ikru urra jtƙa:b Ra:r finnas

'The young goat plays only with its mother.'

u:t aħla:s ihfam uRju:l

'Beat the saddle & the donkey understands.'

(Agram Mostapha)

GERMAN TRADITION

1. **Germany**

When we think about Germany, the first image that comes to mind is that of World War II and the '*Fuhrer.*' In fact, Germany is much more than that. Germany is a country of central Europe. It has a beautiful nature, with its Black Forest, big rivers, modern cities, with its some 80 million inhabitants and long (sometimes-belligerent) history. It has produced many great men such as Goethe, Schiller, Beethoven, and Einstein. It produced great contributions to philosophy and psychology such as *gestalts* psychology (Glossary).

2. **Goethe**

Amongst its most famous figures, who contributed to universal culture, is Johan Wolfgang (Von) Goethe (1749-1832). He was a great poet, playwright and literary theorist. Amongst his most famous works are *Faust* and *Eastern Divan.*

> *Närrisch, dass jeder in seinem Falle*
>
> *Seine besondere Meinung preist!*
>
> *Wenn Islam Gott ergeben heißt,*
>
> *Im Islam leben und sterben wir alle!*

3. German

The German language belongs to the Germanic family (Gleason). It is mainly spoken in central Europe. It is nowadays one of the major languages of the world. It is inflected with four cases (nominative, accusative, genitive and dative), has three genders, two numbers, and strong and weak verbs. German syntax leans towards SOV word order.

German linguists

Amongst the most famous German linguists and philologists were Paul, Schleicher and Grimm. Grimm is responsible for the principle of consonantal shifts in pronunciation, known as Grimm's Law (1822). He held that the nature of the language of a nation was determined by its *sprachgeist* or *volksseele* - 'genius of the language', 'race-soul' – these and similar terms were used more or less interchangeably.

According to Sampson (1980), 'the first question raised by German scholars was whether linguistics is to be considered a *Geistwissenschaft* or a *Naturwissenschaft* – an 'art' or a 'science'.

Most German linguists of the 19th c. worked as philologists within the strait jacket of the Darwinian paradigm. According to them English, German and Norwegian descended from proto-Germanic. The outcome of their works was 'the regimentation of languages into families (Germanic) and supra-families (indo-European). In fact, the term 'indo-European' refers to the family of languages to which English and most languages of Europe and northern India belong. From the proto-indo-European language (PIE) descend Sanskrit, Latin, Greek, and proto-Germanic languages.

According to them, the language which has the most sophisticated grammar is the purist, most original, oldest, nearest to the source, because grammatical inflections and endings are eroded in the development of new languages. English is simpler than Icelandic and German simpler than Gothic.

Their (fittest) 'ease theory' faces problems though, as it says nothing about initial consonant clusters in German, for instance. Initial /k/ as in *knie,* are still pronounced unlike English knee. []'. German consonant final devoicing; the /t/–/d/ opposition is neutralized in word-final position.

In 1880, Hermann Paul could still insist that the historical approach to language was the only scholarly available for linguistic study, despite his disagreement with his predecessors was based not merely on a different view of social phenomena, but on novel presuppositions about the nature of science in general. 'Utility (Zweck) plays the same role in the evolution of linguistic usage'.

'The *stammbaum*, or 'family tree', theory of linguistic evolution was first formally expressed by August Schleicher (in his *Compendium*, 1861.' In fact, 'language must be treated in terms of the psychology of individual speakers, rather than in terms of a *sprachgeist* having some kind of existence above and beyond individuals.' Schleicher was wrong, too, in assuming that if Darwinism was to be applicable to linguistics, then languages had to be seen as genetically-determined living organisms.'

In what concerns connection between language and the theory of 'survival of the fittest,' men do not choose in those terms but rather choose in terms of new fashion and political and economic power!

GRIMM'S LAW: A REVIEW OF THE KING JAMES VERSION

1. The Bible

The Bible consists of two sections, viz. The Old Testament (The Torah) and the New Testament (The Evangels). This is the oldest book in the world and *the* best seller. Its original languages were Hebrew and Greek. It was translated into hundreds if not thousands of languages, including Latin (Jerome, 4 AD), English (King James Version, 1611) and Arabic. The Old Testament consists essentially of Moses' Pentateuch, while the New Testament consists essentially of the four canonical gospels, plus the letters of St. Paul.

The usual attitude of the average Muslim towards this book is 'let me go and burn it!' and the same drastic attitude is found on the Christian side 'Muhammad? – the anti-Christ!' (sic). In this article, I feel somehow optimistic to try and bridge this gap – if not abyss.

This is a critical analysis of different aspects of the Bible as far as its *contents/language* (phonology, syntax, symbols, idioms, parables and stories) are concerned. My major references will be the King James Version of the Bible (henceforth KJV) and the Contemporary English Version of the Bible (Henceforth CEV).

2. English

The English of the KJV is described in the back-cover as 'easy-to-read, self-pronouncing, favorite for almost four centuries (…) It brings the extraordinary power and poetry of Scripture into life.' As far as I am concerned, KJV is not easy-to-read as it includes quite a few linguistic idiosyncrasies in terms of phonetics, syntax, story-telling, etc.

Let us begin with 'the Story of David' in Kings 1:1: "Now King David was old and *stricken in years*, and they covered him with clothes, but he *gat* no heat. Wherefore his servants said unto him, *let there be sought for my lord* the king a young virgin: and let her stand before the king, and let her cherish him, and let her lie in thy bosom, that me lord king may get heat. So they sought for a fair *damsel* throughout all the coasts of Israel, and found Abishag, a Shunammite, and brought her to the king. And the damsel was very fair, and *cherished* the king, and *ministered to* him: but the king knew her *not*."

This story poses a few social and linguistic problems. The enormous difference in age between a 'very old man' and a 'very young damsel' may be considered as illegal in some secular countries. David was so old that he was cold all the time in spite of all the blankets they put on him in the warm climate of the Middle East! He had reached senile age with all its effects of impotence (in some Bible versions, he could not have sex with her) and amnesia (he did not know her). He was so old that he could not even go to the coronation feat of his beloved son Solomon. From his bed, he ordered that his son should ride his mule for recognition.

As far as linguistic idiosyncrasies are concerned, you may have noticed that KJV language is rich and interesting. It was written in so-called Modern English, i.e. Shakespearean English.

The difference between this language and Contemporary English poses a few problems to the linguist.

3. Grimm's Law

If language is the goal and focus of all linguists, the schools and approaches to this subject are many, viz. structuralism, functionalism and philology (also known as diachronic linguistics). A German philologist of the 18th c. called Jacob Grimm suggested a linguistic mechanism known after his name as Grimm's Law to try and deal with the historical development of ancient languages.

To explain philological transformations such as those found in KJV, Grimm's Law which, concerned with consonants, is suggested side-by-side with so-called Great Vowel Shift which is concerned, as its name suggests with vowels. To understand these two theories, one may humorously quote the Mad Tea Party in which each guest is asked to move one place to the right. In language, there are natural tendencies to search for the easiest pronunciation possible i.e., the 'theory of the least effort'. This search for 'least effort' will raise a few problems in language development. Grimm's Law and the Great Vowel Shift (GVS) will try to explain them.

Historically, English belongs to a small linguistic family, i.e. Germanic family (which includes German, Scandinavian and Dutch) and to a bigger and higher family, known as Indo-European, which also includes Sankrit, Hindi, Gujrati. So this has tempted many linguists and philologists to try the reconstruction of the phonetic system of the mother language.

The Germanic branch of Indo-European languages has undergone certain phonetic transformations and thus caused the split between the West and the East in terms of language. Original phonemes such as [bh] [dh] [gh] became [b] [d] [g] first, then [p] [t] [k] and finally [f] [θ] [h]. The following are illustrative examples:

Indo-European	English
Bhero	bear
Ghans	goose
Dekm	ten
Genos	kin
Pater	father
Treyes	three
Kornu	horn

The other set of phonetic transformations concerns the vowel system viz. GVS. In this process, all long vowels lose two degrees in their tongue-height and are transformed into open mid-high diphthongs e.g. [i:] into [ay]:

Illustrative examples are:

Middle English	Modern English	
na:m	neim	'name'
me:t	mi:t	'meat'
ri:d	raid	'ride'
bo:t	boat	

In this story of 'push and drag!' front vowels such as [a] will be substituted for back vowels such as [o]. This is clearly noticeable in verse 'David gat no heat' (spelt with an [a]) and is found in the official motto of the US Dollar 'In God we trust' (cf. Tyneside in England) (cf. Mad Tea Party).

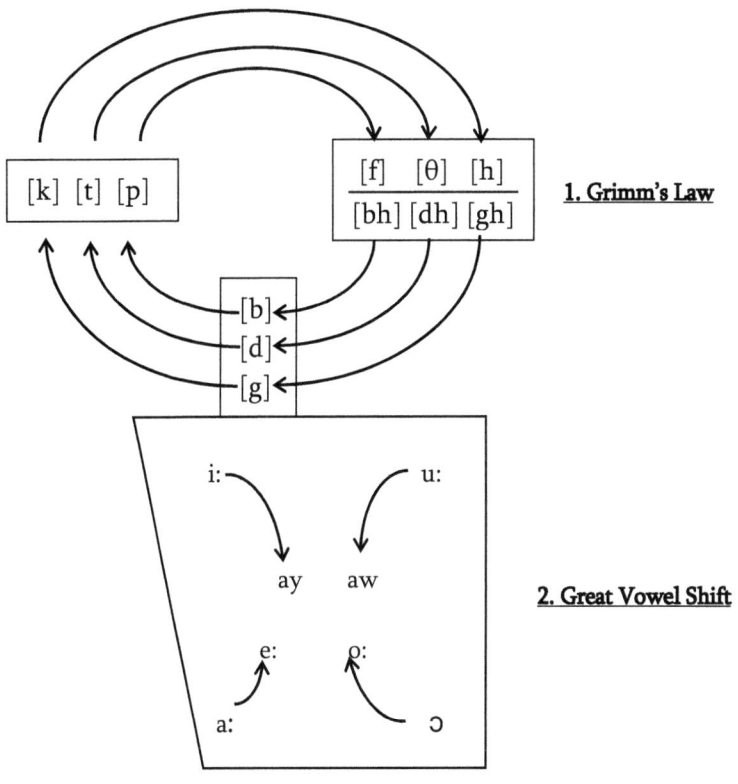

Originally English was a nebula of different languages, viz. Latin, Norse, German, French, etc. (besides being divided into Old, Middle and Modern English).

Latin left words such as 'Bible', 'Pope', 'London', German left 'men and women' (plurals in –en) by opposition to French plural-endings in –s e.g. 'table/table-s'. French also left 'cuisine terms' including 'mutton, beef, poultry'. In David's story we notice words such as 'damsel', 'cherished', 'minister' (someone to serve you!)

Among the syntactic features of KJV is the use of archaic pronouns such as 'thou', 'ye', etc. The use of obsolete linking words such as 'the, and, but', and the use of polysyllabic words such as 'stricken' (struck), 'unto' (to), auxiliary-subject inversion, e.g. 'Then shall the kingdom of heaven belikened unto ten virgins' for 'the kingdom of heaven shall be...' (Matthew 25). The use of passive as in 'let there be sought for my lord'. The use of relative clause such as '*they that were foolish*' for '*the foolish ones.*' The use of *italics* for emphasis and capitalization inside the sentence after a comma or semi-colon. The use of end-negation 'he knew her not', instead of he did not know her'.

Among the stylistic features of KJV, we find the use of parables such as the Story of the Ten virgins (for modern 'girls') (see below). We find also the use of symbols such as 'camel', 'patching', 'fruit', 'song', etc. The 'camel entering the eye of the needle' illustrating the impossibility for a rich man to enter heaven (Matthew 19:24). The ugliness of 'patching an old material with a new one', i.e. defending truth with falsehood: "No man putteth a piece of new cloth unto an old garment, for that which is put in to fill it up taketh from the garment, and the rent is made worse" (Matthew 9:16). In Matthew 21:43 we read: "Therefore say I unto you, The kingdom of God shall be taken from you, and given to a nation bringing forth the fruits thereof. In Isaiah 42:10 we read: "Sing unto the LORD a new song, and his praise from the end of the earth, ye that go down to the sea, and all that is therein; the isles, and the inhabitants thereof."

4. Idioms

Idioms are also used for illustration. For example, when the Roman governor uttered: 'I wash my hands off it', he was expressing the end of his responsibility concerning the execution of Jesus, which was much wanted by the Jews. (Matthew 27:24).

SAUSSURE (I)

Years ago I read an article entitled "*les barbus ne sont plus un taboo.*" It referred to Charles Darwin, Marx and Freud. These modernist thinkers have added more stress to mankind than they helped it. Darwin gave Hitler, Marx Stalin and Freud the permissive society. You may ask what does this have to do with our subject matter? In fact their leader Charles Darwin managed to influence all fields of human knowledge and behavior, biology, morality, religion and indeed language studies.

Darwin is a famous English biologist with his 'struggle for life and survival for the fittest' and his 'Evolution through Natural Selection' theories developed in his book *The Origin of Species.* Let us see what made him most influential in 19th c. Europe, in spite of his scientific failure.

First , Darwin wanted to go from England to Argentina to carry out his experiments (before he could take the boat he had a few problems with the captain who would, years later, confess that he did not want to take Darwin because he did not like the shape of Darwin's *nose*!!). Then from Argentina, he went to Australia because he heard of an Australian ancestral family that buried all its dead in the same cave.

What Darwin wanted to show is the continuity of the different phases of evolution through which some creatures have gone to reach the last stage, which is *man*. According to his hypothesis, life started in water in the form of a simple cell. Then this cell evolved with time until it reached the most complex living organism which is *man*.

In Australia, his experiments consisted of comparing the chain made by the skulls of that Australian family and a chain made by monkey skulls. He tried to work out the similarities and differences between these two chains. But eventually, he could not link the two ends: the monkey chain and the human chain. He was left with a gap between the two and hence the famous term: the *missing link*.

Darwin still included the subtitle 'and the Origin of Man' to the title of his book *Origin of Species,* insinuating that some monkey evolved and became a human being; although strictly speaking his hypothesis was broken by the MISSING LINK.

Scientifically, Darwin failed because of the Missing Link but, he could achieve a tremendous success as far as a new and influential ideology. His theory succeeded in becoming a kind of universal ideological *umbrella covering* East and West: scientists, philosophers, literary men and even the man in the street started talking about natural change, development, evolution.

Beside the missing link, there are a few other critical arguments that could be leveled at Darwin's theory. Neo-Darwinists no longer use the old-fashioned methods of Darwin. They no longer observe and compare old bones and skulls. They are now dealing with nuclear acids and genetic characteristics like the BLUEPRINT. This new genetic principle states that 'one species cannot cross to another even if they are very close.' A lion family, for instance, will always give birth to little lions and never to little tigers. Animals are strictly determined by the genetic BLUEPRINT. So, Darwinism itself has evolved, as it were, and given what is known as Neo-Darwinism.

Nowadays, there are two powerful groups of people in America. Those who still believe in Darwinian *evolution* and those who believe in CREATION. The last group (–) are mostly staunch Christians. They call themselves the 'MORAL MAJORITY'. They say that they 'are fed up with those who have corrupted America.' They believe that these have had their chance to rule or ruin America and that it was 'high time that the people of God ruled American', (sic) to put it in their own words. The Moral Majority believes in CREATION, that is, the world was created by God. Whereas Darwinists believe that the world was created by accident, and to explain life you take Darwinian *evolution*.

The strange thing, however, is that the theory of evolution in its modern version seems very close to that of creation. What Darwin established was a continuous (?) line starting with the simplest phase of life, which was the cell that lived in water and ending with the most complex form of life, which is the human being. To put it in the form of a diagram you would have the axis of time and the axis of evolution and a curved line showing the progression from the simplest to the most complex creature (with, of course, the break known as the *Missing Link*).

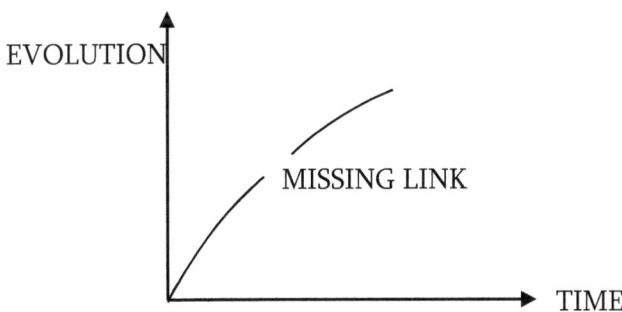

Now, the Neo-Darwinism diagram is no longer a curved line with a Missing Link. It has the form of a BROKEN STAIRCASE.

That is, there are as many missing links as there are (of) creatures, which is very similar to what CREATION says. It states that some creatures are more developed than others, but there are no hereditary links between them. MAN is superior to the other creatures, and no monkey or donkey needed to develop and to become MAN. Each one is quite happy as he is.

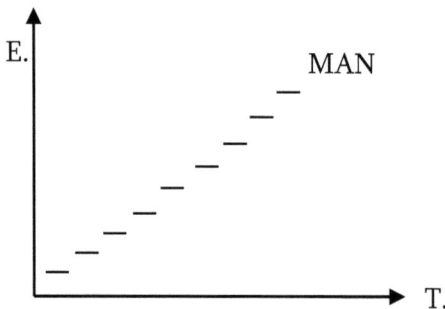

The fourth argument against Darwin's theory is his own concept of *struggle for life* and *survival for the fittest*. This can be put differently. Perhaps there is struggle for life but DESTRUCTION for all. Notice that Hitler was the strongest man of the twentieth century. He could have become the master of the world. He managed to kill millions (some assert that World-War II caused the death of 50 million people). But where is Hitler now? Destroyed.

So it is not struggle but COOPERATION that can allow survival. It is the group whose members cooperate that survives. When you observe nature you see many counter-examples to Darwin's struggle: the alligator always has his teeth cleaned by a little bird that feeds itself from the food swallowed by the big and dangerous animal. The giraffes and the elephants cooperate also to mention only these. (cf. Walker).

Struggle for Life and Survival for The Fittest followed to its logical end should leave us with elephants only since these are the strongest. We find that this is not the case. The elephant lives side by side with the weakest animals. He is even willing to cooperate. So it is not *struggle* but *cooperation*.

Finally, the last argument that could be leveled at Darwin's theory comes from a neighboring discipline, which is that of Physics. Instead of evolution (improvement), as an answer to 'life', Physics suggests something totally opposite i.e. ENTROPY.

For *Entropy* things do not evolve and become better with time; they worsen as time elapses. Nowadays the earth, water and air are polluted with chemicals and nuclear waste. A century ago, the things were much purer. If you just follow the stream of water from its source to the sea you notice that water does not improve the further it moves from its source!

Entropy postulates that the sun as an enormous burning mass has exploded to give the earth, the moon and other planets. It will continue in its exploding and deterioration until it reaches the ABSOLUTE ZERO of temperature.

So according to Entropy, things do not evolve with time; they worsen. There is no improvement, there is continual decay.

Because of these arguments we can say that Darwin has failed. Nevertheless, he succeeded as far as ideology is concerned. Unfortunately, he has given to the modern world a universal ideological umbrella. It is generally accepted by both the East and the West when Europe used to be divided.

Darwin had further succeeded in making a PARADIGM for all scientists to follow including linguists. He had become the model not only for biologists but also for philosophers (remember NIETZSCHE with his *Man and Superman*, which influenced in turn politicians (see Hitler with *Mein Kampf* racist doctrines.

The Germans were considered more evolved than other races, and therefore liable to destroy the other nations for their 'vital space.' Darwin succeeded in fathering literary men and literary interpretations. In linguistics he had his big influence on the movement of HISTORICISM represented by Paul, Schleicher and Otto Jespersen. The latter being the Danish who wrote the best grammar of English: *Essentials of English Grammar.*

The linguist who broke (with) the Darwinian Paradigm was FERDINAND de SAUSSURE. The latter actually established a new approach to linguistics called STRUCTURALISM (perhaps even a new ideology).

He suggested a few notions for the benefit of the modern linguist, which may be divided into two sects: DICHOTOMIES and UNITARY CONCEPTS.

His well-known dichotomies are DIACHRONIC-SYNCHRONIC, *LANGUE / PAROLE*, PARADIGMATIC / SYTAGMATIC and *SIGNIFIE / SIGNIFIANT.* His unitary concepts are ARBITRARINESS, SOCIAL FACT and the most important of all STRUCTURALISM.

He first rejected the hocus-pocus historicist work that he calls the DIACHRONIC approach to language, which was interested in comparing two stages (at least) in the 'life of a language'. Languages were considered somehow like living biological creatures.

For instance the study of the difference between the English of Shakespeare and that of George Orwell. A diachronic study would compare different stages a given language has gone through.

English learners are familiar with the discrepancy which exists between the spelling and the pronunciation. Words like *meet* and *meat* when pronounced the same (both are: mi:t). The diachronic linguist would tell you that when the English language was written these two words used to be distinct and hence their difference in spelling, but with time and evolution (?) they emerged into one another in pronunciation.

Another example of evolution is witnessed between Moroccan Arabic and classical Arabic. Consider the following.

Xaraja	*Xraj*
daXala	*dXul*
Daraba	*Drab*

For Saussure, the linguist should play down the time dimension and study the linguistic phenomenon in the time zero, preferably the present time, as it is used by its speakers. To achieve a SYNCHRONIC study is to be in the same time with the phenomenon you study, like studying modern English as it is right now; and try to find its present structure. The history of English is totally irrelevant to the people doing shopping or restaurants in London-Oxford Street!

After rejecting Diachronic studies, Saussure drew a distinction between *LANGUE & PAROLE*. He, first, cleared away what is not proper for linguists, the concrete side of language and suggested that what we should focus upon is *LANGUE*, that abstract structure behind the words and utterances we can hear or see.

Sociology works similarly. It draws a distinction between student X (the concrete person you can see, hear and shake hands with) and the *Moroccan Student*, an abstract entity to be studied.

Likewise in Language, you can easily see the difference between what the man in Oxford Street! can understand if you utter *car* or *automobile* and what he cannot understand and that is the abstract notion of SYNONYM which holds between the two words. So PAROLE is what you hear and see; LANGUE is an abstract STRUCTURE behind it.

The third Saussurean dichotomy is PARADIGMATIC vs SYNTAGMATIC. PARADIGMATIC is a vertical relation, whereas SYNTAGMATIC is a horizontal one. So in a structure like p i t, and i, e, u, a, ...

$$p \begin{Bmatrix} e \\ a \\ o \\ u \end{Bmatrix} t$$

form a PARADIGM, whereas p - t + any item of the above PARADIGM would form a SYNTAGM. (The paradigm is what the teacher usually calls the table of SUBSTITUTION).

Syntagmatic and paradigmatic relations are found also in syntax. For instance, S V O is a Syntagm, whereas items like *he, my friend, the old man standing in the corner*, etc. form a paradigm: anyone of them can be inserted in the subject position.

_____ V O

The last dichotomy is that of *SIGNIFIE/SIGNIFIANT*. For a word like *glass* we have the following:

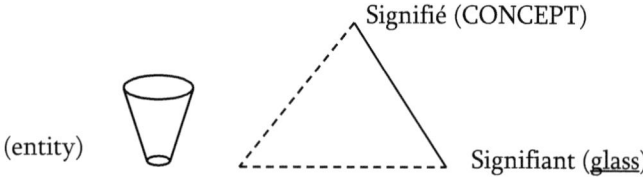

(entity)   Signifié (CONCEPT)

Signifiant (glass)

The usual mistake is to take the material entity for the SIGNIFIE. For Saussure SIGNIFIE is the concept you have in mind about the material entity which may differ from one speaker to another.

Besides dichotomies, Saussure suggested a few unitary concepts. The first one is ARBITRARINESS. For him, the link between 'signifié' and 'signifiant' is ARBITRARY. It is neither natural nor logical, otherwise how would you explain – argues Saussure – that different languages have given different 'signifiants' to the notion *soeur*.

Arbitrariness could be understood when you accept with Saussure that language is a SOCIAL FACT (vs. biological entity). It is agreed upon by society, whatever it is.

What Social Fact also means is that no native speaker can claim to represent his language in its totality, because language is SOCIAL. It needs all the members (all the specialities) of the community to represent what Saussure calls *LANGUE*.

Second, by SOCIAL we mean that language can stand in contrast with say PHYSICAL and PSYCHOLOGICAL facts. Consider what I call 'the story of the usual shop.'

The Usual Shop

Suppose you are used to get your milk and bread every morning from the same shop. You were so used to it that you ended going there 'blindly' not looking.

Unfortunately, one morning you were repulsed while trying to enter that shop. You found a wall built in the place of the door. You could not possibly enter; it is a physical barrier.

This was one possibility. Another one is a mouse for a woman. Women are supposed to be scared by mice. So that woman who was used to get her milk and bread from the same shop every morning would be repulsed from doing so because of a mouse. Obviously, the mouse is no physical barrier. It is not a wall or a lion or even a dog, but the woman could not enter. We say that she was prevented by a psychological barrier.

Now the one but last possibility is to found the sign 'no entry' or the 'one-way traffic' sign. Again you will be reasonably prevented from entering the shop. This time the barrier is neither physical nor psychological. It is social.

Language is social. One last possibility, instead of the nice shopkeeper you were used to, you found a nasty person who would utter the combination of the speech sounds 'go away!' It is a social barrier. English society made those sounds combined as they were mean what they meant: a barrier.

According to Saussure language is a social institution.

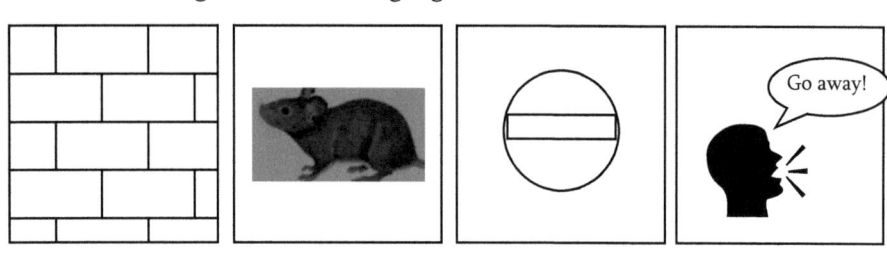

A social fact also means that Mr X, although a Scottish, would not be able to teach with a 'skirt', since one society and societies in general do not allow the male to wear female dress but not vice versa (for some reason!).

Finally, we come to the major contribution of Saussure, namely STRUCTURALISM. To understand it let us put it in contrast with two other and different approaches: HISTORICISM and ATOMISM.

Consider an entity like a *table* for instance.

For the historicist, it was a seed, then a tree, then a set of board and finally it became a table; not to talk about its becoming just dust in a few decades. He is interested in tracing its origins and comparing its different stages.

An atomist, on the other side, would like it to be *golden* instead of *wood* (greedy!). He is interested in its substance, not solely in its shape (FORM or STRUCTURE): *a flat surface supported by legs*; so that it can play the functions of a table, help you have a meal or write on it.

For the structuralist, the ENTITIES do not matter. What is important is the RELATIONS between these entities and the fact that they make a SYSTEM; a STRUCTURE.

According to the social structuralist, it does not matter whether you are a good or a bad person, what matters is the system in which you are caught.

Applied to linguistics, STRUCTURALISM would not give any value to a word unless it is placed in a system. Like the word 'glasses' has no value unless you put it in its syntactic structure:

Either

1. _____ of tea.

Or

2. The teacher is wearing new _____.

Even a fake word like *arara* can become meaningful if I put it in a structure.

1. *arara* chased a mouse.
2. I bought a fish for *arara*.
3. *arara* likes milk.

You have deduced what *arara* means.

Finally, STRUCTURALISM is the basis of all sciences including modern linguistics. It has paved the way to the two main trends in modern linguistics: FUNCTIONALISM (Prague, London) and GENERATIVISM (Chomsky's T.G.).

SAUSSURE (II) : COURS DE LINGUISTIQUE GÉNÉRALE

Ferdinand de Saussure is considered 'the father of modern linguistics'. He had so many innovative contributions that he could influence so many linguists who came after him. One may ask: how was his life? And what were his contributions to linguistics?

1. Life and Books of Ferdinand de Saussure (1857-1913)

Although linguistics existed as a science as early as the beginning of the nineteenth century, Ferdinand de Saussure, born in 1857 in Geneva, son of an eminent Swiss naturalist, is generally regarded as the founder of modern linguistics. Saussure's *Course in General Linguistics* is the most important of all linguistic works written in Western Europe in the twentieth century. Yet it was first published only after his death and was an edited version of notes taken by his students of lectures he gave in Geneva between 1907 and 1911. After having spent ten productive years (1881-91) teaching in Paris (before returning to a chair at Geneva, where he remained until his death), Saussure became increasingly perfectionist, and this prevented him from presenting any treatment of linguistics in the form of a book, since he found it impossible to write anything at all, on such a difficult subject, which he regarded as worthy of publication. This combination of modesty and painful consciousness may explain why he produced only two books in his lifetime, both of them when he was still young, and both in comparative and Indo-European grammar, and not in theoretical linguistics. His first book, published in 1879 when he was only 21, was written in Leipzig while he was attending the lectures of two important Neogrammarians, Leskien and Curtius. His brilliant insights into the vexed question of the Indo-European resonant brought him immediate fame. The second book was his *"doctoral dissertation"* (1880), and was concerned with the absolute genitive in Sanskrit.

2. Saussure's Contributions in Linguistics and his Influence on Linguists' Thought

Saussure's major contribution was to theoretical linguistics. Yet, his writings on the subject were confined to the ***Course***, and then only in the introduction, in Part 1, *'Principes généraux'*, and in Part 2, *'Linguistique synchronique'*, the remainder of the book, albeit suggestive, not having enjoyed equivalent fame. His theory was characterized by the famous distinctions he introduced, which were adopted later by all linguists, and by his conception of the *linguistic sign*.

After distinguishing the study of all social institutions from semiology, as the study of sign systems, then semiology itself from linguistics, and finally the study of language in general from the study of specific human languages, Saussure arrived at the three distinctions which have deeply influenced all linguistic thinking and practice in the twentieth century.

First, *langue* versus *parole*, that is, a distinction between, on the one hand, language as a social resource and inherited system made up of units and rules combining them at all levels, and, on the other hand, speech as the concrete activity by which language is manifested and put to use by individuals in specific circumstances. Saussure stated that linguistics proper is linguistics of language, even though we may speak of linguistics of *parole* and despite the fact that the use of speech alters language systems themselves in the course of history. In fact, he considered only linguistics of *langue* in the *Course*.

Second, *synchrony* versus *diachronic*. Saussure repeatedly emphasized that linguistics, like any other science dealing with values, must embrace two perspectives. A synchronic study is conducted without consideration of the past and it deals with the system of relationships which is reflected in a language as a collective construct. A diachronic study deals mostly with unconscious historical change from one state to another.

Third, *sytagmatic* versus *associative* relationships: a syntagm is defined as a combination of words in the speech chain, and it ties together elements that are effectively present, whereas the relationship called *associative* by Saussure (and, later, paradigmatic by Hjelmslev) unite absent terms belonging to a virtual mnemonic series. Thus, the word *teaching* has an associative relationship with the words *education, training, instruction*, and so on, but a syntagmatic relationship with the word *his* in the syntagm *his teaching*. Saussure added that the very best type of syntagm is the sentence, but he said that sentences belong to *parole* and not to *langue*, so that they are excluded from consideration. This attitude, although consistent, was to have serious consequences for structural linguistics, as it is the reason for its almost total neglect of syntax.

(El Mourabiti Abou El Kacem)

DANISH TRADITION

> 'The simplicity we look for in a scientific theory is something like fewness of elementary concepts employed; and in this respect Lamb beats Chomsky hands down' (Sampson 1980, p.172)

Language X stays language X whether it is spoken, written or transmitted by Morse. According to Saussure, language is 'structure non substance'. The sounds belong to the physical world (acoustic) and the concepts belong either to the physical world or the logical world. The sound repertoire and the concepts repertoire are unstructured. Each language imposes its proper structure on them. Arabic for instance lacks the /v/ sound /s/ and /s/ are contrastive, whereas /b/ and /p/ are not. In English *cousin* expresses the relations of 'son of uncle', 'daughter of uncle', 'son of aunt', and 'daughter of aunt'.

According to Hjemslev, language branches into form and substance on the one hand, and content and expression on the other. These levels combine to yield four 'strata' (layers): substance-content, substance-form, expression-form and expression-content. The extremes do not belong to language.

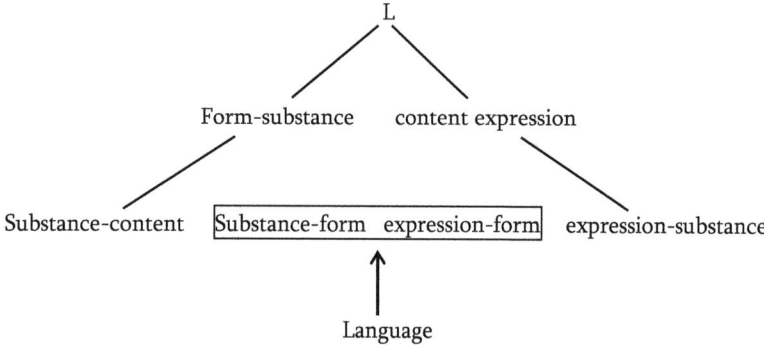

This is pure theory. American Sidney Lamb has tried to make it more concrete by applying it to English. The word LOCOMOTE for instance can be realized as *go* or *move*, which make up a 'sememe'. Likewise *under* and *beneath* (lower position) are alternative realizations of the same semantic element 'lower than'. We can use either one. This is what Lamb calls 'or-relation'. 'Or-relation' is opposed to 'and-relation.' 'Undergo' (submit) for instance consists of 'under' (lower position) and 'go' (move). It is what he calls 'and-relation.'

The 'relation portmanteau' is realized when verb 'go' for instance is combined to 'the first person singular present' to yield 'I go.' It is 'and-relation' and is represented by a triangle, whereas the 'or-relation' is represented by an upside down parenthesis.

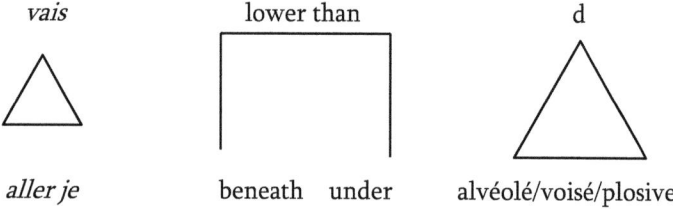

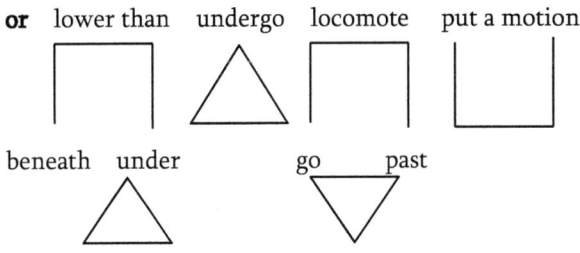

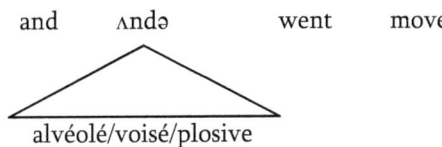

This can be simplified as follows:

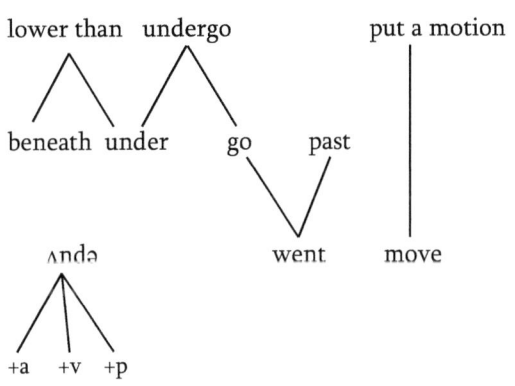

Or again:

A lexeme like *garçon* is a portmanteau for the sense units MALE, YOUNG and HUMAN on the one hand, and the units of sound /g/ /a/ /r/ /s/ /ɔ̃/ on the other.

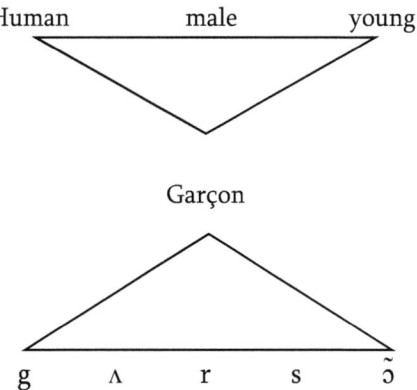

Generally speaking, language connects the messages (semantics) to pronunciation (phonetics). Language offers alternates (or-relation) but the speaker has to choose those which are compatible with the successively larger units. For instance /l/ in Arabic can be either clear or dark depending on the preceding vowel, respectively by /i/ or /a/ and /u/.

Sidney Lamb's theory can find support from new discoveries in computing and aphasia. It is based on the 'item and arrangement' approach. Still, in spite al his efforts to make Hjelmslev's glossematic theory more concrete, American Lamb could not keep up with the Chomskyian school as he based his approach on 'item and arrangement', whereas Chomsky based his on 'item and process.'

Although, Sampson's verdict is that Hjelmslev's idea is a good one, it is unpractical.

Hjelmslev's Glossematics may be regarded as the Saussurean emphasis on form as vs. substance in the 'content plane' (semantics and grammar) and in the 'expression plane' (phonology), and on the definition of form as the interpretations of elements, both carried to their logical extremes; that is to say, content analysis must be independent of extra-linguistic existential criteria, and expression analysis (phonology) must be independent of (assumed extra-linguistic) phonetic criteria. Relations between elements, not the elements themselves, are the object of a science, and only by keeping this strictly to the fore can the Saussurean ideal of an autonomous linguistics, not dependent on any other discipline, be realized. The two planes are each regarded as analyzable into ultimate constituents (e.g. *mare* into m, e, ə or m, a, r, e, on the plane of expression, and into 'horse', 'female', 'singular', on the plane of content). They are not isomorphous, as no connection can be drawn between the individual phonemes or letters and the minimal elements of content; but both planes are to be analyzed in an analogous way, and each is co-ordinate and equivalent in a language system. It is precisely this claim to equivalence between the two planes that others have found difficult to accept, since differences in expression are independently observable in a language and belong to a strictly circumscribed field, whereas differences in semantic content (which is limitless) are only revealed through differences in expression in a language.

Glossematics is a system of linguistic analysis based on the distribution and interrelationship of glossemes, the smallest meaningful units of a language, e.g. a word, a stem, a grammatical element, word order, or an intonation. Glossematics is a theory and system of linguistic analysis proposed by the Danish scholar Louis Hjelmslev (1899-1965) and his collaborators, who were strongly influenced by the work of Swiss linguist Ferdinand de Saussure. He was the leader of the Danish school which was influenced by Saussure who claims that 'language is form non-substance'. He in his turn distinguished the form and the substance of language in expression/form-expression/content. This remained a mere theory until American Sidney Lamb tried to apply it to English. According to him each word is a symbol and is a portmanteau for sound and meaning, e.g. *boy* is /b+o+i/ and [+human+male+adult].

When compared with Chomsky's enterprise, he seems to side with Lamb. He states 'Lamb's treatment of meaning is no worse, though it is no better than Chomsky's.' (Sampson, 1980, p. 169) 'Chomskyan linguists have been forced to recognize the existence of what have been 'conspiracies', in the sense that the outputs of a given bloc of rules manifest patterning which is present neither in the inputs to that bloc of rules nor in the rules themselves (Permutter 1970, p.174). 'Lamb and Chomsky agree in seeing a language as linking 'semantic representations' – messages – with 'phonetic representations' – pronunciation.

FUNCTIONALISM

1. Prague

In this chapter, I want to introduce the Prague school of linguistics, which some people like to consider as more interesting than even Chomsky himself!

Prague, also pronounced /preig/ but this is a rare pronunciation, so we will stick to Prague with the long back vowel. Prague is the name of a city, for those who do not know it yet. It is the capital of Czechoslovakia; so it is behind the Iron Curtain. For most intellectuals, that is Europe, if you say Prague, their minds go to what is referred to as 'the Prague Spring' or *'le printemps de Prague'*: that is the time when the Russian army invaded Prague in the sixties like Afghanistan now.

As far as linguistics is concerned, Prague stands for a special philosophy of language. (We are not doing only linguistics. It's sometimes more philosophical than linguistic. Take for instance STRUCTURALISM; it's not just a linguistic approach. It's also a philosophy not to say an ideology. For some people it's the answer to life. Structuralism is their conception of life.)

Unlike Saussure, who stood alone as the initiator of structuralism, the Prague school consisted of many people; many imminent linguists came to make the Prague school of linguistics. One should mention the founder of that school the Czech Mathesius, the major figure of that school who is the Russian prince Nicolai TRUBETZKOY, another Russian who has turned American Roman Jakobson (spelt/zakobson/), the French linguist André Martinet and finally the native American, to distinguish him from Jackobson, William Labov (shwa, back stressed vowel). So you can see that Prague, as far as linguistics is concerned, does not stand for anything local. It is nothing nationalistic, nothing racist, different people from different nationalities have cooperated to make this school.

Or to put it differently all those scholars who shared the same view and the same method came into being a school called Prague even when they are originally thousands of miles apart.

Once more one has to refer to Saussure as it is considered to be the father of modern linguistics since he has influenced all those who came after him. Saussure considers language to be a social fact. Language is the fruit of society; but Saussure is solely interested in language; the way language is made. Society is, to take another metaphor, "the mother of language" but Saussure's interest is in the "child". For the people of Prague, all students of Saussure, the interest is in both. They consider language as the fruit of society but are also interested in knowing the role played by language in society. LANGUAGE & PEOPLE; not just language like Mr. Saussure. So while Saussure is a pure structuralist Prague people are FUNCTIONALIST.

Prague people looked at the function, the 'use' of language in addition to its 'shape' and 'structure'. While Saussure looked at language as a system, Prague added two other dimensions. They took into consideration people and literature, i.e. the social, the poetic functioning with Roman Jakobson.

Let's consider now the Prague people and see their respective contributions.

We said that this school was founded by Mathesius who was Czech. The main thing attributed to him is this philosophy of FUNCTIONALISM. That is they considered the use of language besides and in addition to its 'structure'. It is used to inform people or to mislead them as it were. Mathesius' famous concept was known as FUNCTIONAL SENTENCE PERSPECTIVE (F.S.P. for short). What does that mean? Take, for instance, a sentence like *Bush has come back*. This sentence brings some (piece) of information. But not all of it is new to you. Half of it is already known to you and hence the reaction. *Bush* is known but what is new is the second half of the sentence 'has come back'.

So for a structuralist, it simply has the structure of a sentence; for Nathesius, it is divided into two halves: the old knowledge you had and the new one. The thing known already is called THEME whereas the new piece of information is called RHEME ('Topic' & 'comment'; '*Mukhbaru bihi*' & '*Mukhbaru 'anhu*'). Of course you need the theme before you could benefit of the rheme. The theme and rheme are like the table and the cup of coffee: you can't put your cup for you until you have a table. So in the case of *Bush* suppose I took another name, a name you did not know; you would not benefit of the information 'has come back'. Again, now that you know that *Bush* has come back, I could add something else and *departed as soon as he had landed*; so in this case the whole first sentence would be the 'theme' and the second sentence *departed as soon as he had landed* would be the 'rheme'.

Now the PASSIVE construction is seen neutrally by a structuralist, but is it so really? Usually, when the government of some country wants to raise the price of some product much needed by the people, they do not say for instance: the minister of economy has decided to raise the prices… They put it in the passive: the prices of sugar, bread, etc. will be raised by 10% starting from next January. So the passive is not just a structure. It plays a role; namely saves the minister from being killed.

The second figure and major linguist of Prague was Prince Nicolai TRUBETZKOY. His father was the dean of a Russian university. He fled from Russia after Lenin took the power. He joined Mathesius in Prague and besides doing linguistics he was doing militancy. At that time Hitler and the Nazis were persecuting people. So Trubetzkoy, who was an open adversary of Nazism and was tortured to death by the Gestapo. He managed to finish his most important book a short time before dying. This important book is known as the Trubetzkoy's PRINCIPLES OF PHONOLOGY.

Trubetzkoy draws a distinction between 3 types of functions in phonology: DEMARCATIVE FUNCTION, DISTINCTIVE FUNCTION and EXPressive function.

First, the distinctive function. Take for example, the three vowels i e o; they would play a distinctive function once inserted in the syntagm p-t. They would distinguish for us between three words that otherwise would remain ambiguous. Those three words are *pit, pet, pot*. and the phoneme, this abstract concept, belongs to LANGUE; whereas the SPEECH SOUND which is concrete merely belongs to PAROLE). (We'll see that this function, namely the distinctive one is carried by Roman Jakobson who uses the distinctive features).

Second, the demarcative function: usually when you drink, if you do it properly, you drink slowly. You don't just pour a jug into your mouth. You empty the glass little by little. As the glass is being emptied, your stomach is being filled little by little. In speech, the same thing happens between the speaker and the hearer. If you are speaking you should respect certain pauses, certain stress patterns, certain sentence rhythms, otherwise you would say things like *dothiko*. Actually, a girl spoke like that. What she wanted to say is I don't think so. You can't understand her, because there isn't enough demarcation in her speech. The opposite could also happen. You may have noticed that some people speak like this: 'hhm... let's see... I mean...' This self-demarcation gives the speaker time to prepare his utterance.

Finally, the expressive function of language or what Le Page calls Acts of Identity, as we will see 'God Willing', means that you have a correlation between different linguistic items and different social considerations. There are relationships between certain linguistic paradigms and certain social facts. Take for instance, the paradigm [au] [eu] [iu] and take the word 'house' we know, that it is pronounced with [au]. But once you go to England, you find that every social group in England speaks a different language. Some would pronounce it with [au], some with [eu], and finally some with [iu]. The lower your pronunciation in the paradigm (scale for London), the lower your social status is. This fact might remind of Bernard Shaw's Pygmalion. Another expressive function of language was noticed by Trubetzkoy in the Mongolian language. (Mongolia has been a country squeezed between Russia and China. In the Mongolian language, there is a difference between the speech of the two sexes. Back vowels in male speech correspond to front vowels in female speech. As I know no Mongolian, I'll use an example from English. Take for instance, the sentence 'I was by the door'; it contains [a]in I, [o] in was, [a] again in by, [o] in door. In the female speech they would be replaced by their front counterparts [a] and [e] respectively.

So we can see that different linguistic items express different social facts.

Roman Jakobson, on his part is a very important figure in functional linguistics. His impact is found on both sides of the Atlantic Ocean. He started in Russia. He went to work with Mathesius and Trubetzkoy in Prague and finished in America as lecturer at 14 Ecole Libre des Hautes Etudes in New York City first, then at Harvard, the most famous university of the United States, at Boston. It is the equivalent of Oxford in England.

Jakobson's fame is due to two major contributions of his: POETICS and UNIVERSAL GRAMMAR. Thanks to these two hypotheses, Jakobson had an immense impact on American scholarship. He first noticed the pragmatic mentality of Americans who look for material, concrete benefits; so they came to idealize science at the expense of arts. In America, if you are in science and technology, you can become rich; whereas if you are a painter, a writer, a poet, etc. you are doomed to starve unlike the physicist, the chemist and the linguist.

To bring a remedy to this regrettable state of affairs, Jakobson proposed Poetics (which is different from stylistics as the latter deals with the different styles of the same language; whereas poetics deals with the aesthetic aspects of language) as a kind of marriage between science and arts, more precisely between linguistics and literature. Those working in poetics try to apply linguistic theories to the analysis of literary texts (Cf. Ross dealt with a poem about 'Jerusalem' and the advertisement of coca Cola).

> Have a coke and smile makes you feel nice makes me feel good ah; that's the way it should be and I'd like to see the whole world smiling with me coca Cola adds life have a coke and smile

We suggest that this sequence should be divided and made into a poem:

Have coke and smile
Makes you feel nice
Makes me feel good
Ah, that's the way it should be
And I'd like to see
The whole world
Smiling with me
Coca cola adds life
Have a coke and smile

Notice the parallelisms in SOUND and WORD, e.g. [ai] which is found in smile, smiling and also the transformation (Nominalization): smile ➔ smiling. The first one denoting life while the second is frozen and makes the action of smiling become a product of the capitalist system just like a coke: have a coke and smile, i. e. the smile is parallel to the coke. Now if you join the parallelisms you obtain the visual image of the smile and that of the coke tin.

Universal grammar, on its side is a theory that suggests that all languages are cut to the same pattern. Again, this theory that Jakobson applied to phonology and which Chomsky would apply later to syntax gave him another theory known as the theory of DINSTINCTIVE FEATURES in phonology and have had an important role in re-orienting linguistics in the USA. American descriptivists, before the advent of Jakobson, thought in terms of RELATIVISM (vs UG). They thought that languages can vary endlessly (there is no limit to the way languages could differ). (For them each language was different from the others).

For Jakobson, languages can vary indeed but within limits which he calls Universal Grammar. We may speak different languages. We may even use different sounds like the [x] sound we mentioned, which exists in certain languages but not in others; but still, we all have the same features like VELAR, FRICATIVE, STOP, etc.. Languages may differ but they are like the fingers of the same hand in the depth. They are just one hand and hence the hypothesis of Universal Grammar.

For Jakobson, it is different. It has to do with the psychology of the individual. Not only do we all share those features like velar, etc... (which shows the similarity of our vocal articulations) but in fact what Jakobson wanted to demonstrate is much more sophisticated than that. He wanted to show the insight that goes beyond the vocal tract of the human mind. Those (twelve) features have a psychological reality and are the same in all human beings.

The human mind is the same for all human beings and this has consequences for the field of CHILD LANGUAGE, too. A Moroccan child taken to China would come to acquire Chinese perfectly after a few years (before the 'plastic age'). The same for a Chinese child taken to England, he would acquire English as his mother-tongue.

Let's take a brief illustration of how distinctive features work. Suppose I wanted to talk about somebody, could you tell who this person is? The answer is no since there are billions of people. Suppose now I made it more precise: an English person. Still no clear answer; there are, we said, some 70 million of them. An English teacher? No. An old English teacher? There are thousands of them. Old English Teacher in this department is just one Mad. So while other phonologists started with the entity phoneme (although the phoneme is a concept belonging to 'langue' and is 'signifié,' Jakobson dealt with the features (the qualities) of the phoneme that described him and no other phoneme, and hence their qualification as Distinctive.

In phonology (after the social example) one could take, say, six phonemes X_1, X_2, X_3, X_4, X_5, X_6 [b] [m] [t] [d] [n] [l]. What do we notice then? We notice that [b] is LABIAL, the difference between [t] and [d] is VOICE; so let's see whether these two properties are sufficient to distinguish our set of speech sounds.

	b	m	T	D	n	l
LABIAL	+	+	-	-	-	-
VOICE	+	+	-	+	+	+

These two features do not seem to help much. Of course, they have set the [t] sound apart. But the others are not: the [b] and [m] are not distinguished yet and likewise for [d] and [l]. Let's move to another trial by adding the features NASAL and see what is going to happen.

	b	m	T	D	n	l
LABIAL	+	+	-	-	-	-
VOICE	+	+	-	+	+	+
NASAL	-	+	-	-	+	-

2. London

England had some spelling reforms in the 16th c., as the English were trying to make their National Language out of the multitude of unintelligible dialects they had at their time (eyren). And this task required a very serious work in PHONETICS. One should also take into consideration, what was known in the nineteenth and beginning of the twentieth century as the BRITISH EMPIRE (up to the 1950s when the subjugated countries started becoming independent and made what is known as the COMMONWEALTH [in association with Britain]. The colonies of the British Empire consisted of countries like EGYPT, NIGERIA, SOUTH AFRICA, etc. In our continent, it consisted also of CHINA, INDIA, IRAQ in Asia. Actually, it consisted of many countries and it stretched from MALAYSIA in the far-east to the INDIES in Central America (the place of bob Marley: Jamaica, Barbados, Trinidad, etc.)

So you can easily imagine the number of languages available to the English linguists working at a school called S.O.A.S (School of Oriental and African Studies), which is a section in London College University; and hence the title 'LONDON SCHOOL'.

The people who made (since most of them have died except for one) London School are Henry Sweet, Daniel Jones, J.R. Firth, Malinowsky and Micheal Halliday. Henry Sweet and Daniel Jones were phoneticians, J.R. Firth dealt with phonology and semantics, Malinowsky dealt with semantics and Halliday with syntax.

Henry Sweet was responsible for the PHONEME. He is the original of Professor Higgins in Bernard Shaw's Pygmalion. For some personal animosity, he never succeeded in having a job at S.O.A.S. as a lecturer, in spite of his work and publications. His merits were recognized only after his death (posthumous).

Daniel Jones was responsible for the CARDINAL VOWEL SYSTEM, (i e a/u o ʌ) and the author of this nice book called Everyman's English Pronouncing Dictionary.

Both Sweet and Jones worked hard on the English SPELLING REFORM, on SHORT HAND and I.P.A. (i.e. International Phonetic Alphabet).

J. R. FIRTH is the major figure of London School. Firth worked in phonology, as I said. He had a special approach to phonology called PROSODIC phonology. Prosodic phonology draws our attention to the fact that the approach based on the phoneme is misleading (let alone normal spelling). The approach based on the phoneme is segmental, i.e. it divides speech into segments VCCV. But with some languages like Chinese (remember China was a British colony) this approach did not work satisfactorily (i.e. nan). As I do not know any Chinese, let us take the preposition, in English, on. Obviously, it consists of two segments (alas two phonemes). But what about the French impersonal pronoun *on*? Does it also consist of two phonemes? The segmental approach is misleading. In fact, it consists of only one vowel with a prosody (o). We do not produce the /o/ vowel then an /n/ separately. In reality we produce them together and the prosody is just a help of the vowel /o/. the nasal feature (represented by a diacritic) just 'colours' the vowel. (This is one of the idiosyncrasies of the French language).

In semantics, J.R. FIRTH questions (as far as the relationship between FORM and MEANING is concerned) the Saussurian notion of 'Arbitrariness'. For him, this relationship is not totally arbitrary. One could try and find the connection between form and meaning. Take, for instance, the words starting with the consonant cluster sl in English; words like slave, slam, slain.. they all seem to share some kind of a negative connotation (feature); namely 'violence'. The slaves were taken violently from their home-land. (Remember 'Roots'). To slam the door means to shut it violently and slain (to slay [ei]) means to kill violently.

Take another paradigm, this time from Arabic. The verb paradigm:

sa:la	*ma :la*	*ta :la*
(to flow)	(to be inclined)	(to be long)

They all seem to connote some kind of continuation of some sort. So it is not just the case of onomatopoeia that justifies the link between form and meaning (*signifiant/signifié*).

Malinowsky, on his part, has mainly dealt with semantics. He worked in the Trobriand Islands), some remote islands that belonged to the British Empire at that time. So he was not only interested in linguistics but in anthropology as well.

So you find some of the books of Malinowsky having the insulting titles like 'The life… of the savages'. If we forget about his prejudices and talk about his purely linguistic contributions, especially semantics, he would link language to culture. Each language is closely linked to its particular culture. You cannot understand its meaning unless you put it back in its context. And the term CONTEXT is very important not only for Malinowsky but for all the members of the London School.

Another semantic concept found with Malinowsky is that the meaning of a sentence could be equated with the observable results achieved by uttering it.

So for instance, stand up! (The student stands up). This is the meaning of the utterance stand up. Look out of the window! (The student looks out of the window); this is the meaning of the sentence look out of the window. This conception of meaning is also found with the philosopher of Cambridge Wittgenstein and is called PERFORMATIVES (the notion of). When a prisoner is executed, one should not look at the hangman and say that the hangman is responsible for killing him or look at the rope! These are just means. They are neutral tools. The one who really killed the prisoner is the sentence: I sentence you to death uttered by the judge. So according to Maliknowsky, as well as to some philosophers like Wittgenstein (Austin Quine, Searle, ..) language is not to 'tell' but to 'do'. It is not 'telling'; it is 'doing'.

Now Michael Halliday is the only member who is still alive; I mean the only founding member, because there are many people who are working within the London frame, especially in teaching and translation.

Halliday is a syntactician. He has a book called 'Syntax and the Consumer'. Notice for 'the consumer' the phrase not just syntax or the syntactic structures. So like the rest of the members of London, he takes into consideration the 'use of language'. Words are 'tolls', one could look at their shape, usually one asks the question 'what for is this?' He looks for the possible 'use' of that tool. Now the tool could be just a screwdriver which needs only one person to use it, or a boat or a plane, in which case you need a whole crew.

Halliday looks at syntax through three dimensions: SYSTEM, RANK and DELICACY (the – scale).

System (and this is a term to remember, as it applies to the whole approach of the school) simply means a set of possibilities (exclusive alternatives), choices or as the teachers of English call it a table of substitution.

So – for instance – in a sentence like 'Mary came home late yesterday', we can substitute 'she'/ 'our neighbour'/ 'the person living next door', etc. for Mary. Those possibilities will be put one above the other between BRACES like this (so the braces are just a notation that is hanging around. It is actually a theoretical (construct) representation. They represent a certain syntactic relation. They are different from the parentheses and the square brackets. Each representation has its own meaning, as we shall see, in spite of some people's confusion about them).

Rank now could be illustrated by an example from biochemistry. The smallest unit in nature is the atom, a few atoms make for you a molecule, millions of molecules make one of your cells, thousands of cells make an organ and finally the organs make your organism, i. e. your body. Or to take an illustration from sociology, you could say that the individual is the smallest (hopefully invisible unit; at least two individuals make a family (the children are optional); families make a tribe especially in the country-side; hundreds of tribes make a nation and the nations of the world make humanity.

In syntax, Halliday suggests something similar to this. That is, you have one rank included in a bigger rank. And he suggests 5 ranks for English: MORPH, WORD, FROUP, CLAUSE and finally SENTENCE. So, for instance, in a sentence like: 'Any gangster trying to ride the stallion will be thrown off'. You have 'gangster' which starts with the morph 'gang'. The morph 'gang' is the first rank. It is included in the second rank which is the word 'gangster'. In its turn, 'gangster' is included in the third rank, which is the group: 'any gangster' (called phrase by other linguists like Chomsky). The group 'any gangster' is included in the one but last group 'any gangster trying to ride the stallion' and finally this clause is included in the largest rank which is the sentence.

Finally, Halliday suggests DELICACY, which means that for instance if I said, "Well look at this picture." (Maggie Thatcher). Suppose I asked you this question: "What's the difference between her and a human being?" We know she is Thatcher. What's the difference between these two words, PERSON and THATCHER? The difference is that one is more inclusive than the other. 'Person' is more inclusive than 'Thatcher' and the latter is more precise than 'person'. 'Person' includes millions of other entities besides 'Thatcher'; whereas 'Mrs. Thatcher' is just one person.

Actually, there is a scale of delicacy. In our case, the scale (or hierarchy) would go from PERSON/WOMAN/ENGLISH WOMAN/ENGLISH WOMAN DOING POLITICS/THATCHER. One item is less inclusive than the preceding one, but at the same time more precise. The higher we go in the scale of delicacy, the less referents there are and the more precise our term becomes.

This is especially relevant for translation; take the example of a student who translated 'خُضَر' (MA) as 'not boiled' (Cf raw). He has gone too high in the scale of delicacy. Because the scale presents us with: not cooked and not boiled (together with other equally possible interpretations like not roasted, i.e. cooked with no oil, no water and not fried/frying).

To go back to the consumer. If you hear from someone this sentence: I have a vehicle, you can guess that he has chosen the lowest item of the scale; can you guess the kind of vehicle? He has probably just a bicycle. Because if he had a Rolce Royce or a *Jaguar* he would go to the highest point in the scale:

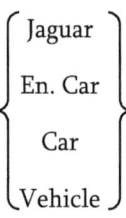

To sum up, the London School is also referred to as SYSTEMIC LINGUISTICS (pronounced /sisti:mik/ although it is written systemic and sometimes polystemic, although it could be referred to Systemic and Contextual. That is because each context requires one (and only one) item from a given system.

```
          S
          Y
          S
    C O N T E X T
          E
          M
```

This approach, consisting of SYSTEM and CONTEXT () is applied by the London people (scholars) to all levels, namely PHONOLOGY, SYNTAX, and SEMANTICS.

First, in phonology, we could consider STRESS and ASSIMILATION both in English and Arabic. Take, for instance, 'Mary came home late yesterday'. Suppose that this were what you knew and suppose that someone said that it was 'John came late yesterday', what would you do? You would protest and show it with much emphasis on Mary: 'Mary came home late yesterday'. Suppose now he said that Mary 'departed/went away', you would stress 'came home' and likewise for 'late' if he said 'early' and 'yesterday' if he said 'two days ago', for instance. So we see that there is a SYSTEM of stress options. Each option applies to a given context (either 1 X Y Z i.e. the context made by the words of the sentence or more broadly by the discussion.)

Now ASSIMILATION: suppose we had the following Arabic paradigm:

من عاد		n	/q
من يئس	$n_n \rightarrow$	j	/j
من كان		n	/k
من تاب		n	/t

We noticed that for each context corresponded one item from the system n/j/n/n (Dental).

In English you have, similarly the paradigm SYSTEM (sometimes to refer PARADIGMATIC as the relationship and SYNTAGMATIC as the horizontal one is misleading. This could be remedied perhaps as PARADIGM is EITHER OR relation and SYNTAGM as AND relation of STRESS). So I said in English ASSIMILATION also works by SYSTEM and CONTEXT. Take for instance these human beings, anglo (WASP) which give you the system:

$$\begin{Bmatrix} m \\ n \\ n \end{Bmatrix} \text{ announce}$$

In SYNTAX the same approach is used that is the SYSTEM/CONTEXT dimensions. Take for instance, the sentence 'Mary came home late yesterday' to pick that one again. It is a syntactic context and allows for systems (at least 4) like:

$$\left\{\begin{array}{l}\text{Mary}\\ \text{She}\end{array}\right\} \text{came home late yesterday.}$$

The same applies at the junction level of the verb:

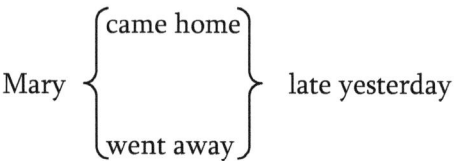

It can apply also at the level of the adverb of manner and time.

In semantics, remember Malinowsky, you cannot interpret the meaning of a sentence without its context. And this bears heavily on TRANSLATION and TEACHING. You cannot translate a text without its context. And you cannot teach a foreign language without its context. As an alternative of sending the learner to England which is the proper context of English, some teachers suggest the alternative of the classroom. And this reminds me of my first experience in teaching. I was given to the supervision of a teacher of English for beginners. He was short and dynamic. He was asking his pupils the question 'What is the teacher doing?' and did the action; they would answer, he is running, he is jumping. I thought to myself would never be able to do it!

As a CONCLUSION: Go to England if you want to study PHONETICS.

3. Robert Le Page

Robert Le Page is a famous linguist thanks to his contributions:

- "ACTS of IDENTITY" which deals with the sociolinguistic problems faced by black minorities in white racist societies (like the case of Malcolm X).
- Computer Aided Cluster Analysis.
- The "Four Riders" or "Four Senses" as explained by Le Page himself:

"The Four senses I have mentioned in which we refer to 'a language', frequently confusing them, are as follows:

Sense One refers to what is felt to be a speaker's native language, or which he uses in his most informal and relaxed behaviour with his peers. William Labov has tried to capture language in this sense, claiming that linguists normally work as informants. I believe 'language' in this sense to be a purely hypothetical construct, a linguistic base – line which the individual needs, but without other justification and certainly inaccessible. Peer-group behaviour is just as much conditioned by my hypothesis and its riders as solipsist behaviour or lame behaviour, the 'me' who is talking to my wife is no more the 'real me' than the 'me' talking to my students, although I certainly take up different roles and these roles have different linguistic symptoms.

Sense Two is what is accessible through performance. It is socially-marked behaviour. It reflects the groups which the individual believes exist in his society and his desire to be identified with or distinguished from them. This SOCIALLY-MARKED DATA is what forms the basis for the learner's creation of his linguistic systems; it is what the sociolinguistic is learning to work with; the linguist and the psycholinguist have yet to recognize it for what it is.

Sense Three is the linguist's descriptive abstraction from the data. It is always partial, and always powerfully conditioned by the linguist's linguistic theories and educational experience. It tends to concentrate on those aspects of language which have traditionally been described – and we owe a good deal to Malinowski, to Firth and to Dell Hymes for helping to rescue us from that particular treadmill. Secondly, it becomes inevitably prescriptive, and provides a powerful focusing agent for the behaviour of educated groups, so that many communities become bilingual or diglossic by virtue of their members needing to show that they are familiar with a particular artefact of an elite in their society. (See De Silva, 1976, 1979).

Sense Four is very similar to Saussure's *langue*. It is inherent in the daily behaviour of a community as well as in its oral or written memory, laws, stereotypes. It can never be fully described, and is, of course, continually changing. Partial abstractions made from time are not always comparable, since they may draw on different members of the community or different modes of behaviour or be cast in different moulds, though it is these partial abstractions which usually constitute the basis of comparative and historical linguistics. There is theoretical continuity of transmission of linguistic models, either geographically or historically from community to community, or from generation to generation or both, but we are not in a position to make a complete inventory of sense four language for any community and the narrow genetic metaphor is more misleading than helpful. I believe that Bickerton's *Dynamics of a Creole System* (1975) is an attempt to describe a language – 'The Guyanese Language' – in sense four, and is extremely valuable for that reason alone, even though the attempt revealed – as I feel it was bound to – the impossibility of the task. Dell Hymes similarly has set linguists an impossible task in calling for descriptions of communicative competence. It is much more complex than describing how to use money; and the latter task has so far defeated economists.

WITTGENSTEIN

Ludwig Wittgenstein was one of the philosophers of Cambridge. Although from Austrian origin, he worked and lived in England. He was one of the positivist (empiricist) philosophers like August Comte and Francis Bacon, and more specifically one of the ordinary-language philosophers like Austin and Quine.

He criticized philosophy bitterly as it has according to him wasted too much time on pseudo-problems, whereas its first task and aim should be to investigate LANGUAGE.

Wittgenstein is considered as one of the best (Anglo-Saxon) philosophers of the twentieth century, who wrote extensively about language and religion. We may rightly ask, 'what are the new things that brought up this philosopher in these two fields of knowledge?'

It is worth bearing in mind that the religion of Wittgenstein's parents was Christianity. His family was wealthy but Wittgenstein himself was not interested in money and preferred to live simply. For him, there are no philosophical problems, but just linguistic confusion. Yet, he had a long life interest in religion and claimed to see every problem from a religious point of view. However, he said in his 1992 *Lecture on Ethics*, that the tendency of all men who ever tried to write about ethics or religion was to run against the boundaries of language. This gave support to the view that Wittgenstein believed in mystical truth that somehow cannot be expressed meaningfully, but is of the almost importance.

Not surprisingly, Wittgenstein wants the reader of his books not to think so much but to look at the language game that gives rise to philosophical problems. Obviously, in a world of contingency one cannot prove that a particular attitude is the correct to take. Thus, the spirit of relativism seems far from Wittgenstein's conversation and absolute tolerance. With regard to religion, this philosopher is often considered a kind of anti-realist, who emphasized doctrine or philosophical arguments intended to prove God's existence, but was greatly drawn to religious rituals and symbols. He had even considered becoming a priest once.

Wittgenstein's way of using the word 'grammar' is a key to understanding his work in philosophy. He said that, 'any explanation of the use of language was grammar,' which includes whatever is needed to describe the meaning of language. For instance, the part of speech 'noun' is defined as the name of a person, place, or thing. Still, Wittgenstein called into question our textbook definitions. To ask for example whether by calling all nouns names of objects, emotions, numbers and so on, we do not cover up profound differences in the ways we use words. And so to ask whether school grammar, and the inferences we draw from it, may lead us to misunderstand the logic of language. If we classify any particular word as a noun, we have already gone some way towards giving the word its meaning. Therefore, according to Wittgenstein, by grammar, we shall mean the rules of using a sign and also the account we give of those rules.

According to Jasper Doomen [p.c.], it is important to know that most interpreters of Wittgenstein's work distinguish two periods: in the first period, he develops a philosophy according to which language mirrors the world: a situation corresponds with a description in words. A famous example is this: Wittgenstein read about a court trial in the newspaper. In this trial, a model car was used to represent the real car. In the same way, a picture consists of elements, each of which stands in a relation of correspondence or reference to some object. This is his famous picture theory.

The book in which he expounds his ideas is the *Tractatus Logico-Philosophicus*, a short work with a great number of theses and sub-theses. Thesis 2.1 (p.14) runs as follows: "We construe pictures of the facts." Furthermore, "the picture is a model of reality." (Thesis 2.12 (p.15)) The picture is a standard of reality (according to thesis 2.1512 (p.15)). "A sentence can only be true or false insofar as it is a picture of reality" (thesis 4.06 (p.30)); "The sentence is a picture of reality" (thesis 4.01 (p.26)).

He appeals to a sort of logical atomism (the philosopher Bertrand Russell defended a philosophy with this name): the smallest parts of language, the atoms, serve as the bases for sentences: "The simplest sentence, the elementary sentence (*Elementarsatz* in German), asserts the being of a state of affairs." (thesis 4.21(p.38)).

He initially thought to have solved all philosophical queries and abandoned philosophy. But in time, he concluded that language is too complex to be merely characterized as the simple linguistic reconstruction of the world. His most important work written after *Tractatus Logico-Philosophicus* is a work called *Philosophische Uuntersuchungen* (Philosophical Investigations), published after his death. This is representative of the second period.

In this book, he is critical of his earlier views. He represents the following example: suppose one is dealing with the sentence 'five red apples'. According to his earlier views, there should be a correspondence between the atomic facts and the world (his earlier view; cf. thesis 4.21 of the *Tractatus Logico-Philosophicus* mentioned above), but he now casts doubt on this view by asking what exactly the five refers to (&1 (p. 238)). It cannot, after all, be pointed out. The same problem comes to the fore when one wants to make it clear that something is not red; to what does one, then refer? Obviously not to something red (& 429 (p. 415)).

Instead of maintaining, as he did in the *Tractatus Logico-Philosophicus*, that language as such corresponds with things, he differentiates between various language games, '*Sprachspiele*' in German (& 7 (p.241)). The language game is an activity or a form of life (& 23 (p. 250)). Rules constitute an important part of this exposition (&54 (pp.270, 271)). In this approach, it is use which determines the meaning of sentences. If one should, for example, want to clarify what a game is, examples are presented. It is not of importance to see a general characteristic in these, but to use them (& 71 (p.280)).

So Wittgenstein's main idea must be answered twofoldly. His main idea in the first period is that one gives an analysis of the world through language; there is a clear correlation between the way the world is constituted and its representation through language. One should not say anything which cannot be said (thesis 6.53 (p.85)). By the way: Wittgenstein states himself, 'It is my main thought, that the "logical constants" can't be substituted. That the logic of facts can't be substituted.' The original German runs as follows: "*Mein Grundgedanke ist dab die" logischen Konstanten' nicht vertreten. Dab sich die Logik der Ttsachen nicht vertreten labt.* (thesis 4.0312 (p. 29)). He sees the purpose of philosophy in clarifying thoughts logically (thesis 4.112 (p.33)).

His main idea in the second period is that there is no common standard for making sense of the world (as he had thought himself in the *Tractatus Logico-Philosophicus*), but that language games are decisive for individual situations and that the application of language is primary.

This approach must be followed in answering the question: what Wittgenstein's opinion about religion is, as well. His opinion about religion in the first period is relatively easy started: religion cannot, according to him, be expressed in language. That is, he does not express atheism, but the subject cannot be dealt with within the limits language poses, 'How the world is, is completely indifferent for the Higher being. God does not present himself in the world." (Thesis 6.432 (p.84)). It is important to know what Wittgenstein means by 'the world': the world is everything which is the case; it is the completeness of facts, not of things. (Theses 1 and 1.1 (p.11))

The mystical can't be expressed; it shows itself (thesis 6.522 (p.85)). He concludes the *Tractatus Logico-Philosophicus* with the famous phrase '*Woveon man nicht sprechen kann, daruber mub man schweigen.*' ("Whereof one cannot speak, one must be silent") (Thesis 7 (p.85)). In the *Philosophische Untersuchungen*, his position is not clearly conveyed.

Wittgenstein was a student of Russell's who had suggested the sentence "the King of France is bald" in a famous and influential article, meaning that: there is one and only one entity that is the King of France and that entity is bald" (thus false, because there is no such entity. In contrast, "The Queen of England is visiting Morocco" would be true or false depending on whether that entity, which does exist, in fact has the property "visiting Morocco." (Chomsky, p.c.)

Bertrand Russell was proud of his student WITTGENSTEIN. He used to say "soon he knew all I had to teach" and called him "Mr. Wittgenstein".

Some of the technical terms used by Wittgenstein among other logicians are synthetic vs. analytic truth, excluded middle, middle term, sophistry, logical connectives. Let us exemplify them in turn.

TRUTH can be either synthetic, i.e. observable, or analytic, depending on reason alone. EXCLUDED MIDDLE is a case of reasoning where you have only two options; nothing in between e.g. All roses are either yellow or red. MIDDLE TERM is the predicate of the major premise and the subject of the minor premise. It is what you delete to obtain the conclusion of the syllogism.

All men are mortal – Socrates is a man – Socrates is mortal. SOPHISTRY is a seemingly sound deduction but is not, such as: All cats eat fish – John eats fish – John is a cat.

Dealing with the Logical CONNECTIVES such as then (implication) Wittgenstein establishes the following Truth Table

It rains. It's wet → If it is raining (then) it will be wet

It rains.	It's wet	If it is raining (then) it will be wet
1	1	1
1	0	0
0	1	1
0	0	1

One case of Excluded Middle and sophistry is found in Caner & Caner (2002, p.18)

If Jesus claimed to be God, he could not have been a prophet.

MARXISM & MARRISM

Marrism is the linguistic theory of the Soviet Union before 1950. It drew on Marxist dichotomy and dialectics of "superstructure" being determined by "infra-structure".

According to Robins (1967, p.224):

"Marr, himself a Georgian by birth and from his early youth gifted with remarkable language learning ability, turned his attention first, like some other Russian scholars, to Georgian and the rest of the Caucasian languages. In investigating the history of the Caucasian languages he gradually evolved his own theory (or theories) of linguistic history. Rejecting the accepted Indo-European theory, he drew his ideas from eighteenth-century beliefs in the gestural origin of language and from middle nineteenth-century opinion on linguistic typology as an indication of stages of progressive linguistic development. The 'Japhetic' languages, a term he used to cover the languages of the Caucasus, represented a stage in the evolution of language through which some other languages had already passed. Languages were historically related, not in linguistic families, but by the different evolutionary 'layers' of structure deposited from continual mixtures and combinations. Languages were not national, but class phenomena, and were part of the superstructure whose changes correspond in the economic base of the speakers' social organization; here he claimed the theoretical alliance of Marrism and Marxism.

Claiming to explain not only linguistic history but also linguistic prehistory by his theory, Marr soon transcended mere observational statements, and declared that the words of all languages could be traced back to four [primitive elements: [sal], [ber], [jon] and [rosh]. Such unsupported theorizing enjoyed official patronage, and several other Russian scholars found it prudent to uphold and even eulogize Marr's pronouncements, until 1950 when suddenly Stalin ordained the rejection of the whole Marrist edifice, pointing out, among other things, that language was not dependent on economic organization since the same Russian language served both pre-revolutionary capitalism and post-revolutionary communism, a statement of the obvious not apparently made before. Stalin's intervention both ended the long reign of Marrist theory and drew the world's attention to it. Since then, with the post-war expansion of international cooperation in linguistic studies, Russian linguists have started to work in closer contact with those of the rest of Western Europe and America, and current western developments are being keenly and fruitfully debated. In general linguistic particular attention is paid to lexicography (...)."

Conclusion: the Russian of the comrades was the same language as the one the Tsar used!!

BLOOMFIELDIANS

According to Drimmer, the author of *Black History*, the white American bears a feeling of guilt because of the Indian Genocide. This feeling pushed many of its intellectuals to try and fix the culture and languages of the Native Americans. The most famous of these were Leonard Bloomfield, Edward Sapir (both authors of books bearing the same title, viz. *Language*), Charles Hocket and Christian missionary Kenneth Pike. The last is linked to Bible translation and the Summer Institute of Linguistics [S.I.L.], which is one of the most active institutes of linguistics.

1. Bloomfield

Leonard Bloomfield was an American linguist whose book *Language* (1933) was one of the most important books of linguistic science in the first half of the 20th century and he, almost alone, determined the subsequent course of linguistics in the United States. Concerned at first with the details of Indo-European languages – particularly Germanic – speech sounds and word formation, Bloomfield turned to larger, more general, and wider ranging considerations of language science in his *An Introduction to the Study of Language* (1914).

He began (1917) pioneer studies of the Malayo-Polynesian (Australo-nesian) languages, especially Tagalong. In the early

1920's, he began his classical work on North American Indian languages, contributing the first of many descriptive and comparative studies of the Algonquian family. In the writing of language, Bloomfield claimed that linguistic phenomena could properly and successfully be studied when isolated from their non-linguistic environment. Adhering to behaviourist principles [of psychology], he avoided all but empirical description. *A Leonard Bloomfield Anthology* was edited by Charles Hocket in (1970).

2. Sapir-Whorf

Sapir Edward, a leader in American structural linguistics, was one of the first who explored the relationship between language studies and anthropology [bad word?] His methodology had strong influence on all his successors.

Later on was developed a theory of language known as the Sapir-Whorf Hypothesis. It advocates that 'language creates thought'. For instance, people behaved cautiously near what they categorized as 'full petrol drums' but carelessly near 'empty petrol drums', although the 'empty' drums contained explosive petrol vapour and were thus even more dangerous than the full ones. There exists also numerous 'covert' categories, or 'crypto-types' as Whorf sometimes calls them. They are learnt by rote. Hopi never borrows spatial terms to refer to temporal phenomena in the way so common in European languages; such as *before the door-before noon, between London and New York...*" (Sampson 1980, p. 81)

Cambridge philosopher Ludwig Wittgenstein in his later writings argued a view very similar to Whorf's (though without Whorf's knowledge of exotic languages).

3. Zellig Harris

Zellig Harris was a renown American linguist and teacher of Chomsky. He was born in Ukraine in 1909. He was a linguist, mathematician and scientific methodologist. He got his Bachelor's in 1930, his Masters in 1932 and PhD in 1934 from the University of Pennsylvania. He began teaching at that university in 1931 and was the founder of the first linguistics department in the US in 1946. His book *Methods in Structural Linguistics* (1951) is the definitive formulation of American descriptive structure linguistics.

Zellig Harris carried Bloomfieldian ideas of linguistic description to their extreme. He recognized, as Sapir and Bloomfield that semantics is included in grammar, not separated from it, form and information are the same thing. His book *Methods in Structural Linguistics* (1951) made him famous but is still misinterpreted as a model of a 'Neo-Bloomfieldian School' of structuralism. He defined transformation as a mapping operation that preserves linear combinations. Harris and Chomsky developed their concepts of transformation on different bases by adapting post-production systems as formalism for generating grammar like symbols' systems. This led to redefinition of a transformation as an operation mapping a deep structure into a surface structure. A sequence of this abstract treatment is that relations between words must be managed by a separate tool for semantics and their phonological shapes by a separate phonological tool.

Harris's writings include *a Grammar of English on Mathematical Principles* (1982), *A Theory of Language and Information* (1991). His works seem to be widely scientific because of his ancient studies, such as *Origin of the Alphabet* (1932),

Methods in Structural Linguistics (1951) and *The Form of Information in Science* (1989). The latter was about the sublanguages of science and meta-language definitions of terms and relations, which restrict word combinability, and the correlation of form with meaning. Other works concern the linguistic history, and structural linguistics such as *Development of the Canaanite Dialects: An Investigation in Linguistic History* (1939).

Finally, Zellig Harris was a great linguist in his field. Moreover, he had many famous students, like Chomsky, Joseph Applegate, Lila Gleitman, Michael Gottfried, Maurice Gross and others.

PIKE (I): SUMMARY OF PIKE'S *LINGUISTIC CONCEPTS – AN INTRODUCTION TO TAGMEMICS* (1982)

An *emic* unit is 'an entity seen as "same" from the perspective of the internal logic of the containing system, as if it were unchanging even when the outside analyst easily perceives the change' (xii).

An *etic* unit is 'the point of view of the outsider as he tries to penetrate a system alien to him; and it also labels some component of an emic unit, or some variant of it, or some preliminary guess at the presence of internal emic units, as seen either by the alien observer or as seen by the internal observer when somehow he becomes explicitly aware of such variants through teaching or techniques provided by outsiders.

Kenneth Pike is against restricted approaches to linguistics and chooses to start in linguistic analysis from social interaction which opens perspectives for studying dialogue, sentence, pronunciation, differences between people in particular and various contexts (xiii).

Tagmemic theory is complex, because it requires considering context 'at every step: that is, in all perception and experience and knowledge' (xiv). This theory is synonymous to *unit-in-context* (xiv).

We may approach things that have some kind of relationship in so many different ways, and while trying to determine the nature of the relationships between them, we tend to look for what is useful, but 'so often, [we are obliged to do so] on the form in which (…) facts are given' (xiv).

Pike wants his theory to be suitable to as many fields and situations as possible and not only to linguistics. 'Human emic experience is the target, not merely linguistics' (xv), he states.

The tagmemic theory came as a result of so many researches and attempts to find as general principles as possible (that would be applicable to a wide range of languages). The theory revealed itself to be even applicable to other fields of research (anthropology for ex.) (xv).

1. The Observer and Things

The nature of a 'thing' depends on many factors: the observer himself, the use or purpose of this thing, the theory adopted by the observer; brief, 'the observer (…) affects the data and becomes part of the data.' (3).

1.1. Theory

Theory is important, because it is what makes practice possible. 'Today's practicality is often no more than the accepted form of yesterday's theory.' (5).

A theory helps in seeing specific data from just one point of view. A theory is helpful only if it is 'simpler than reality.' (5). It becomes simple when it discards what the observer does not have to consider on the spot, so as to enable him to get answers to particular cases.

A model is much useful as it allows studying more easily what reality actually holds without facing the difficulty of directly dealing with reality.

Pike considers the existence of a theory necessary. A good theory 'leaves out wisely' (6) what is not pertinent to the resolution of the problem studied. When the problem has been resolved – in a way, a new theory is needed so as to include more factors and thus be more useful. Those factors should normally be those left out by prior theories (7).

Building a theory is a process in which one would 'seek an organized, systematic arrangement of general principles which will help (…) to *understand* something about our physical or conceptual world.' 'A theory may be viewed as a conceptual tool.' (7). The quality of a theory depends on its usefulness, that depends in turn on the goal behind it. 'A theory is most likely to be useful if its results, or predictions, can be easily tested.' (8).

The inductive method: this method starts from the data and moves towards the theory.

The deductive method: this method starts from the theory and moves towards the data.

Using the *inductive method* means that the researcher is going to gather as much relevant data as possible and apply it to the guessed at large pattern, and then verify its validity.

Using the *deductive method* means that the researcher starts from a number of premises that he builds on his observation of data, taking into account the way those premises were arrived at.

The use of many theories helps reaching more interesting results and may lead to corroborating one another's results, i.e. arrive to one (to some extent) complete overview (9).

1.2. Survey of Tagmemic Theory

It is impossible to build a theory or start a scientific investigation without holding certain truths for granted. However, research shows that many beliefs may be challenged with the evidence of new facts.

Tagmemics also starts from a number of premises and assumptions. 'It helps to suggest the relevant structures arrangement of behavioral units relative to an insider's (emic) view of a behavioral system.' (11).

Tagmemic theory asserts the existence of at least three perspectives used by man who deals with three-dimensional experiences. The first dimension is that of chunks and segments: PARTICLES. The second dimension is that of merging things and levels of hierarchy: WAVES. The third dimension is that of simultaneous characteristics added to the experience and making up its pattern: FIELD (13).

A unit is known by its uniqueness that comes from its specific features that make it always different from other units even when changes happen to it. It is well known when its right place is also well known.

In language for example, there are different kinds of hierarchies that we experience while using or interacting with language: First, the grammatical hierarchy: parts within larger parts within still larger parts (affixes, words, phrases, clauses, sentences, paragraphs, speeches…). Second, the phonological hierarchy:

sounds within syllables within stressed syllables within stressed groups of words... Third, the referential hierarchy that makes language use dependent on many factors such as the purpose, the situation, the speaker's perspective and so many others (15).

Treating language as behavior and within its social context, not apart from it, makes it possible to give language a meaning. 'Language elements are combinations of form and meaning.' (16).

A universe of discourse is not determined by the words used in it but rather by the socially intelligible relationships between them. Discourse links language and society (18).

1.3. Particles

Particles are items as we see them in our daily experience. They may constitute real physical objects, or groups of objects, or abstract concepts. Although many of these may not be exactly single, distinct, very precise items, we tend to consider them as particles, as this is the way the mind deals with them (19).

In language, we can consider as particles: sounds, words, clauses, phonological patterns (such as in limericks). In the case of a clause, there are possibilities concerning the functional objects that constitute it. Each of them may be treated as a tagmeme particle (21-23).

Particles as we experience them daily and as we perceive them, are arranged sometimes in a linear way (one following the other), and sometimes spatially, with a kind of relationship or state. The spatially ordered particles are within a field (23).

1.4. Wave

In speech, sounds are not uttered separately. They are merged in the previous and the following ones. Before the first sound is finished, the following one begins already. This is how speech is intelligible. The merging of sounds into sequences constitutes a wave (24-26).

In a sound sequence, there is a nucleus (the clearest and steadiest part) and a margin (the transition from one sound to another). Nuclei are particles, while the flow movement (margin, nucleus, margin, …) is considered to be a wave (26).

Kinds of waves (27-28):

A **grammar** wave is a wave in which a distinction between nucleus and margin is made concerning constructions: stem and affix; phrases; clauses (dependent/ independent); questions/ answers…

A **phonological** wave is a wave in which a distinction is made between nucleus and margin: stressed/unstressed syllables; emphasized words within a phrase or a sentence; emphasized sentences within a speech – similarly.

A **referential** wave is related to reported events, exposition and argument, in which the nucleus is the climax of the story or the most important point of the exposition, while the remaining parts can be considered pre-marginal and post-marginal.

A wave of meaning is related to the meanings given to words in various contexts. There is, however, a central or basic meaning that we may call the nucleus, in comparison with the 'off-norm' (28), figurative, highly contextual, idiomatic meaning that we may call the margin.

By extension, we may talk about waves when dealing with anything that bears a clear distinction between a nucleus and a margin (whether spatially or chronologically) (29).

1.5. Field

A field is the 'total set of relationships and of units in these relationships' (30).

Units are meaningful only when interpreted by an observer as having a meaning within a context (involving the observer's point of view and the context, which determine together that meaning). The relationship with field is that context itself is within a field (30).

Different sounds have some common features in which they can be said to intersect. The set of relationships between different sounds constitute a field; a field of various dimensions of relationships (31-33).

Clauses have relationships of dependence/independence, of transitivity/intransitivity, which have intersections when a number of languages are studied. The relationships and intersections have many dimensions within this field: the structure of clauses (33-36).

Verbal cues used by the observer while analyzing may suggest whether he is considering the object of study a particle, a wave, or a field. Still the same object of study may be considered differently with the shifting point of view of the observer and may even be combined in some cases.

2. The Unit

2.1. Contrast and Identification

We always tend to recognize units by determining what they are not, what differences they have with other units that make them what they are, unlike all others. Yet, determining that nature of a unit requires to differentiate it from units that are similar (share common features with them) but not the same as them. Both contrast and similarity enable identification and are based on field and the observer's interest (42-43).

It is more difficult to differentiate two units that are very similar. Sounds for example give meanings, and the slightest change may largely affect meaning. In very similar conditions, we are more likely to spot this difference (between one sound and another in a context) (43-44). Contrast is thus closely related to meaning and context.

'Language is not merely a set of unrelated sounds, clauses, rules, and meanings; it is a total coherent system of these integrating with each other, and with behavior, context, universe of discourse, and observer perspectives.' (44).

Matrices of different kinds (three-dimensional, columns and rows...) help finding more features of a system and making contrasts (47-49) (languages, clauses, sounds, meanings, etc.).

When some words are uttered in an identical way, it is only the context that enables contrast and identification. In non-verbal communication, contrast shows that the same gesture may have two different interpretations in two different cultures (49-51).

2.2. Variation

The identity of a unit needs to be clear enough to enable considering it the same unit despite any change that may occur to it and affect it. The question is: what are the features that may change (vary) without causing the loss of identity of the unit (52)? From an inside point of view, it is easy to recognize the way the native speaker would pronounce them. Tagmemic description targets then the inclusion of more criteria of differentiation (54).

Even tiny changes in pronunciation, in the stressed words within a sentence, in speed, affect meaning and are '*crucial signals of style*' and other social behavior indicators (54-55).

Grammatical variation: when the grammatical structure remains the same while different words can be replaced by substitutes that fill the same function, we call it free variation. Some *free variations* however, would result in a *conditioned variation* as in the example in which the plural is replaced by the singular or vice versa. In other cases, the placement of some words, either at the beginning or the end of a sentence is '*locally free*, but *focus* – or *style* – or *discourse-conditioned*' (56). Abbreviated variants are another example. Poetic or classical language variations are yet another example (free and conditioned at the same time) (56).

'It would be convenient to have some unique term which refers to variants of all kinds of units (both phonological and grammatical). A solution is to call a variant of any emic unit an all-unit (from a Greek word meaning 'other'). Thus we can have *allophones* or phonemes; *allomorphs* of morphemes, *allomatrices*, and so on.' (56).

In a sequence, it is hard to perform segmentation, because we cannot know where exactly the first part ends and the second begins. When a sequence is considered as a wave, it does not really count, but when the particle is to be analyzed, segmentation is necessary, but dependent on the analyst's perspective and objectives rather than on data itself (75-59).

2.3. Distribution

Units (persons, things, words, etc.) are distributed in such a way as they belong to groups or classes relevant to their identity and which are in turn within larger universes of discourse. Units are characterized by their membership in classes of interchangeable items within kinds of structures (62). Units are also characterized by structured sequences (mainly grammatical).

A word is significant within a structure and a context in which it plays its role(s), as a person is identified in society by his place within its structures and by the roles he plays in it (62).

Sounds are also identifiable within a sequence, as part of it. The distinction of the same sounds differ from one language to another, as certain sequences of vowels and/or consonants are possible in a language but does not occur in another (63).

A unit can also be defined 'by the place it fills in a matrix of units.' This place can help even in contrasting units. 'The distributional relation of a unit to a background system must enter the definition of every unit.' (65) (In addition to other features).

3. Hierarchy

3.1. Grammatical Hierarchy

Pike asserts that hierarchy (small parts within larger parts within still larger parts) 'is an important component of our approach' (70).

In language, it is easier to hear a limited number of words and understand them at once. We hear and understand in chunks. They are largely dependent on and affected by meaning on the one hand, and have functions in behavior; language is society and context-bound (72).

The ***unit-in-context*** (the Tagmeme): 'the four features of a tagmeme are in part independently variable; they are also mutually dependent on each other, with interlocking components and definitions.' (75).

(1) Slot	(2) Class
Where (the position)	What (the items)
Specific place of part in whole	General set of items substitutable appropriately in the slot
Wave characteristic, with nuclear or marginal relation	Particle characteristic
Syntagmatic relations	Paradigmatic relations
(3) Role	(4) Cohesion
Why (the relevance)	How tied to other units
Specific function of the set to other sets in the including whole	General background materials from any level of the hierarchy which are controlled by or controlling the item in view
Behavioral meaning	Field characteristic, systemic structure
Pragmatic meaning	Framework relations

'The unit-in-context (the tagmeme) has interlocking features, each quasi-independent, but each dependent on all of the others. Hence the unit in view here is not the isolated lexical item, but a set of elements and features of elements mutually relevant – hence the term unit-in-context.' (75).

3.2. The Phonological Hierarchy

Phonological segments are hierarchically ordered, but with different sets of hierarchies, related to the syllable, the stress group and the like. Those hierarchies determine the kind of relationship that exists between sounds, syllables and stress-groups, and the kind and degree of dependence among them (84-86).

Emic comes from phonemic, while etic comes from phonetic. They are not clearly distinguishable when uttered within relatively long chunks, when they occur within waves. The author makes at this point the difference between nuclear and marginal units as he moves through the phonological hierarchy: *phone, syllable, stress group, phonological paragraph, phonological discourse, utterance and response* (89).

Intonation highly affects the way the utterance is interpreted; a difference of intonation may lead to opposite interpretations of the same utterance. This applies also to poetry in which intonation is crucial to meaning, although some teachers prefer to leave the interpretation to the reader, regardless of intonation (93-96).

3.3. The Referential Hierarchy

The referential hierarchy, in contrast with the grammatical and the phonological ones, is concerned more with the content, the meaning or event. 'The telling about an event [is more independent] than the mention of a name of something.' (98). A related event belongs to a higher level of the referential hierarchy than the items involved in relating it (98).

In a certain context, a given lexical item may be paraphrased in many ways without losing its identity. This is a referential identification (related to the context that enables to preserve the identity of the item despite its changing form) (98).

A higher level of the referential hierarchy is the fact that an event could be part of a larger event, in turn part of a still larger event, as we could have two (or more) separate events that meet and merge into one event at a given point. 'Such merging event complex also serves as a unit of the referential hierarchy analogous to the complex sentence (or even higher unit) of grammar.' (99).

The referential tagmeme involves, like the grammatical and phonological ones, slot (where), class (what), role (why) and cohesion (how). The role or purpose of an event highly depends on the context of that event and the interpretation of the viewer/hearer, based on the event itself, on its place or relationship with other events... (100). As to slot and class, the event under analysis is not studied in isolation with the events before and those after, as it is considered a choice among many other possibilities (a set of paradigms). As to cohesion, it is controlled to some extent by the expectancies of the hearer and the speaker, and by the rules that the kind of exchange requires (100).

A sentence might be grammatically correct, but according to the frame of reference false. Hence 'A statement can be factually correct, or true, even though badly stated. And a lie can be elegantly framed by a con man to cheat a victim.' (105).

The frame of reference is important in understanding (speaker and hearer). If it differs among speaker and hearer, they might not understand each other (105).

4. Context

The author insists on keeping form and meaning together and never isolating one from the other. He emphasizes the idea that change always occurs within a framework. Higher-level frames and universes of discourse are given importance in this part as well.

4.1. Form and Meaning

Pike considers it an impossibility the existence of a form (of a unit) without a meaning (got in any way and from any source), and the existence of any meaning or significance without a form that shapes this meaning or gives it its 'physical manifestation' (111).

'The substance shared by grammar, phonology and reference we call lexicon.' (112)

'Meanings in language as used by the man in the street are treated as features relevant to behavioral impact, including the elicitation of understanding' (112). 'Each of the units manifesting each level of each hierarchy carries some kind of behavioral impact.' (112).

Form and meaning intersect in hierarchies (grammatical, phonological and referential) at different points in each case, as the diagram shows (for the detailed diagram see p.114):

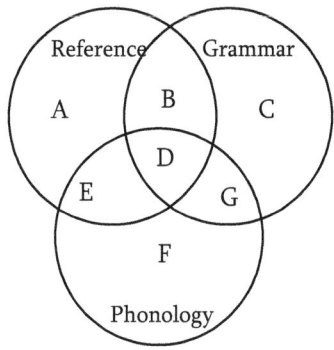

Thus, 'Tagmemic theory affirms that language contains and is composed of emic form-meaning composites' (117).

4.2. Sharing as Prerequisite to Change

In a sound sequence, change may occur to some sounds as they merge into one another to form this sequence, and result in a new shared sound. The shared element may be a whole word or words (or parts) in a sequence that sound the same, but which force a change from one meaning to another.

When it comes to the meanings of a word, a marginal meaning may share an aspect with the context and change accordingly. 'A change in meaning-viewed-as-wave is forced by its shared context, whether that is physical, mental, social, or linguistic.' (120).

Change from a central meaning to a marginal one is forced by context and social convention (121). 'No change [occurs] unless something contextual [is] shared.' (126).

4.3. Universe of Discourse

Discourse is the "*frame of reference*" (126) 'within which social interchange is taking place.' 'It can include topic, style, genre, discipline, or general speaker or hearer expectancies.' (126).

The lack of coherence in speaker-hearer interaction results from the lack of a common or shared background or system of belief, and may lead to 'conversational chaos' (127).

Despite all kinds of differences between cultures and languages, there are common 'behavioral universals' that they all share, such as the basic survival needs, the 'roles differentiation, communication, shared cognitive orientations and goals, and regulation of disruptive behavior, as well as means of socialization…' (131).

Translation is assumed to be possible despite all cross-cultural differences and obstacles. Context always plays a vital role in giving meaning. Even an exact translation of a word is insignificant without a contextual framework that enables the receiver to make sense of it (132).

The author argues that the definition and meanings of a word are derived and inferred from the various contexts in which this word occurs and the way the speakers use it. Thus, the meanings of a given word change to fit new discoveries, certain areas of discourse, new contexts and cultural exchange (adaptation) (132).

The tagmemic theory's 'crucial assumption' is that 'personal interaction is given priority over identification of things or abstractions' (136).

Further, 'the theory must be able to *describe* any one variation of interaction, after it has occurred, without being forced to predict in advance which one must inevitably occur.' (136).

Pike, Kenneth Lee. <u>Linguistic Concepts – an Introduction to Tagmemics</u>. University of Nebraska Press, Lincoln & London. A Bison Book: 1982.

(Soumia Ben Rochd)

PIKE (II): SUMMER INSTITUTE OF LINGUISTICS [SIL]

Kenneth Pike was a famous figure in linguistics, especially in North Texas, as he taught at the Summer Institute of Linguistics (SIL) headquarters and was a personal friend of many students and faculty members of the UTA linguistic program. Besides his being a great linguist, Pike was well known for his Christian missionary work, about which he wrote many influential books that continue to serve as inspiration to SIL. Pike's intellectual orientation is both linguistics and religion.

1. Life

Pike was born in Woodstock, Connecticut, and studied at Cordon College, from which he graduated in 1933. He initially wanted to do missionary work in China. When this was denied to him, he went on to study Amerindian languages at the SIL in 1935. He then joined the university of Oklahoma, to learn Mixtec () from its native speakers in Mexico. In 1937, Pike joined the University of Michigan, where he worked for his doctorate in linguistics under the supervision of Edward Sapir. Pike obtained his PhD in 1942, and became president of SIL. This institute's main function was to produce translations of the Judeo-Christian Bible into unwritten languages. In 1951 Pike published the *Mixtec New Bible*. He was promoted president of SIL international from 1942 to 1979. He was also a member of the National Academy of Sciences, the Linguistic Society of America and the Anthropological Association (). He was nominated for the Nobel Prize for his work in linguistics.

2. The 'emic'/ 'etic' Theory

Pike is best known for his distinction between 'etic' and 'emic' aspects of linguistic investigation. 'Emic' (as in phonemics) refers to subjective understanding and account of meaning in the sounds of a language, while 'etic' (as in phonetics) refers to the objective study of sounds. In fact no one can be totally objective and 'etic' in any study. Everyone bears his own 'emic' subjective perspective! Pike further argued that only native speakers are competent judges of 'emic' descriptions and are thus crucial in providing data for linguistic research. The investigation from outside applies scientific methods in the analysis of language, producing 'etic' descriptions, which are verifiable. Pike himself carried out studies of indigenous languages in Australia, Bolivia, Equator and Java.

3. Tagmemics Theory

Kenneth Pike's theory, called *Tagmemics* focused from its early inception upon solving the problems; which the translators of the Bible faced in understanding and describing languages of pre-literal cultures. Pike and his wife Evelyn have had considerable influence on the development of Tagmemics discourse theory. They devised practical tools of inquiry for identifying and charting similarities and differences in alien languages lacking alphabet and grammar. Pike soon understood that the problem challenging translators laid both beyond the sentence, in discourse and beyond discourse itself in the socio-cultural framework in which the target language is spoken. Pike and his colleagues thus began building a theory of discourse based upon the centrality of language in human communities.

In Tagmemics terms, a rhetorical task involves deliberately leaving behind a default 'etic' or outsiders perspective on data under consideration and employing heuristics that assist a communicator in approximating an 'emic' or insider's perspective – reaching the audience live!

4. Pike and Religion

Pike was not only a great linguist but also a Christian missionary. Throughout his long career, he was interested in the religious aspect of linguistic studies and worked in close relation with Wycliffe Bible Translators. Pike with others linguists such as Angel Merecias and Donald Stark completed the translation of the New Testament into the San Miguel Mixtec in 1951.

Besides this, Pike was a Christian philosopher and a convinced theist who attracted thousands of people towards the Christian religion. He wrote numerous articles and books, such as *With Heart and Mind*, in which he defended the scholarly approach to Christianity, stating that Christian faith and academic scholarship can be intimately integrated. Once Hugh Steven said, 'to understand and appreciate Pike, one must know that he was both a scholar and a Christian, that his faith in Christ was at once full of energy without pretence and rooted in biblical depth.'

Kenneth Pike was a renowned figure in American linguistics. By suggesting his 'etic' and 'emic' Tagmemics theory, he has helped many linguists in solving the problems that translators faced with the text of the Bible. The duality 'etic' 'emic' is set "on the basic assumption that there is always an 'observer perspective' on the data. There is no such thing as a detached, impartial perspective on any data…' (Linda Jones 1995)

According to Sampson (1980) Pike's work has a 'very concrete practical purpose: to aid the conversion of the heathen by enabling the Holy Scriptures to be given to every human in his own mother tongue. The Summer Institute of Linguistics provides linguistic training for the missionaries of the Wycliffe Bible Translators, Inc., founded in 1949, who are working with the very numerous and wholly alien vernacular languages of large parts of central and south America and of the western pacific area. Such languages invariably lack a writing system, let alone any pedagogical tradition.'

To sum up, Kenneth Pike was a renowned figure in linguistics by stating his 'etic' and 'emic' theory, which has helped many linguists and Bible translators. The Tagmeme (unit-in-context) approach stresses the fact that 'language is not merely a set of unrelated sounds, clauses, rules, and meanings; it is the total coherent system of these integrating with each other, and with behavior, context, universe of discourse, and observer perspectives.'

Pike considers it impossible the existence of a *form* without *meaning*, and the existence of any meaning without a form that shapes this meaning or gives it its 'physical manifestation.'

LABOV'S SOCIOLINGUISTICS

William Labov was born on December, the fourth of the year 1927 in Rutherford, New Jersey. He studied at Harvard in 1948 from which he got his BA and worked as an industrial chemist from 1949 to 1961 before turning to linguistics. His Master's thesis was about the change in the dialect of Martha's Vineyard, which was presented before the Linguistic Society of America to great acclaim.

Then, Labov received his PhD degree from Columbia University in 1963. He taught at Columbia from 1964 to 1970 before becoming a professor of linguistics at the University of Pennsylvania in 1971, which has become the Mecca for the discipline, and he became the director of the university's linguistic laboratory in 1977. The methods he used to collect data for his study of the varieties of English spoken in New York City, published as the social stratification of English in New York City in 1966, have been most influential in social dialectology.

In the late 1960s and early 1970s, his studies of the linguistic features of African American Vernacular English (AAVE) were also influential. He argued that AAVE should not be underestimated as substandard but respected as a variety of English with its own grammatical rules, although speakers of AAVE should be encouraged to learn standard American English for interactions in society at large. He is also famous for his seminal studies of the way ordinary people structure narrative stories of their own lives.

William Labov has been the dominant figure in sociolinguistics since its emergence in the mid-1960s. He studied with Weinreich who was the head of Columbia Department of Linguistics. Through this native Yiddish (Hebrew dialect, Labov was exposed to the most progressive view of language extant in classical linguistics, its variability and changeability across space, time, speakers, domains and contexts. With Weinreich, Labov laid down a program for the empirical study of language in the speech community in 1968, thus making the bridge between the traditional study of language and the new field of sociolinguistics.

In fact, his 1963 Master project on a sound change in progress in Martha's Vineyard and his 1964 PhD thesis on sociolinguistics stratification on the New York City introduced Vernacular English in Harlem, starting in 1965, that he made the paradigmatic breakthroughs underlying the modern field of linguistic variation theory.

Labov's intent was an empirical, rigorous, and reproducible approach to language as it is actually used, a scientific linguistics. His ambivalence about the label 'sociolinguistics' reflected his overarching project of advancing linguistic theory by grounding it in solid data and objective analyses rather than unverifiable intuitions and polemic debate, without sacrificing the creative roles of scientific insight and intricate inductive and deductive reasoning.

This program was carried out by Labov, his students and disciples worldwide. It has met with undeniable success. The principles of sound change he established and the universal and language-specific constraint hierarchies he discovered have had a great impact on phonology and other areas of linguistics. His studies on /t/-/d/ deletion, auxiliary contraction, and other aspects have been replicated many times and have served as models for entire research traditions in New Worlds: Spanish, Canadian French, Brazilian Portuguese, and other languages. However, despite its unwavering focus on the linguistics of spoken language, or perhaps because of it, the intellectual power of this approach, studying usage instead of intuition, and concentrating on the elucidation of linguistic structure in social and historical context rather than using predefined language features as tools for properly social science investigations, it has also revolutionized many other disciplines within language science.

His long-standing interest in the vowel system of American English, particularly the northern cities shift and the relationships among English dialects worldwide, has profoundly changed dialectology. Based on his experience in urban speech communities, he was able to dramatically increase the social validity of survey studies, while introducing new techniques and technology to increase efficiencies and to multiply the kinds of discovery possible. This work culminated in the monumental Atlas of North American English, whose computer-based methods have transformed dialectology.

Labov made many contributions to the analysis of narratives. While his deep insights into the transformation of everyday experience into narrative would be hard to rival, the example he set, and the protocols he established for the analysis of narrative discourse have inspired a proliferation of research in this area. In the study of social change, Labov's gender and class-based models of language variation change remain fundamental for the understanding of the prestige and influence of sociodemographic groups, culturally-specific gender roles, and the modeling and quantitative dynamics of trait diffusion within the community.

As a conclusion, his work includes *Language in Inner City, Studies in Black English Vernacular* (1972), *Sociolinguistic Patterns* (1972), and *Principles of Linguistic Change* (2001). Together with Sharon Ash and Charles Boberg, he produced *The Atlas of North American English* (2006).

(Ramdani Meftah)

CHOMSKY'S TG GRAMMAR

'If we are satisfied that an apple falls to the ground because that is its natural place, there will be no serious science of mechanics. The same is true if one is satisfied with traditional rules for forming questions, or with the lexical entries in the most elaborate dictionaries, none of which come close to describing simple properties of these linguistic objects.'
(Chomsky)

1. Chomsky's Life

Noam Chomsky was born in Philadelphia in 1928. He is an American linguist and honorary professor of linguistics at the Massachusetts Institute of Technology from 1955 until now. He is considered the founder of transformational linguistics. On his many travels, he introduced himself to the public as a committed intellectual with a liberal socialist tendency and anarchist.

Chomsky began developing his theory of generative-transformational grammar in the 1950s, aiming at going beyond the structural, distributive, and behavioral approach of the Bloomfieldians. To account for the innate structure of language, this theory is often described as the most important contribution to theoretical linguistics in the twentieth century. Some speak of the Chomsky Revolution (such as Smith and Wilson from the

University of London). In response to criticism against his first model in the 1970s, Chomsky proposed a new version of his theory based on a normative approach in the early 1980s. In the 1990s he laid the groundwork for what he called the "The Minimal Program."

Chomsky's research played a decisive role in the so-called "cognitive revolution." His criticism of Skinner's *Verbal Behavior* in 1959 marked a revolution in the study of language and the mind since the 50's. This corresponded to a great response in the philosophy of language and the mind. He also founded the Chomskian Hierarchy, a method of classifying formal languages according to their generative power.

In addition to his academic career, Chomsky has been engaged in intense militant activities since the mid-1960s when he spoke out against the Vietnam War. He has his sympathy going to the trade union movement of which he is a member. He has given a number of conferences around the world and published many books and articles presenting his historical, social and political analyzes. His criticism focuses specifically on US foreign policy and the media.

In 1992, Chomsky was the most cited academic according to the Humanities Quotation Index, and was ranked eighth on the list of the most authoritative authors. Chomsky is an important intellectual figure in today's world, arousing controversy and admiration.

2. Phrase Structure Grammar

The Bloomfieldian linguists dealt somehow with syntax; their approach was known as the Immediate Constituent Analysis (or IC analysis for short). For instance, in an "Indian" utterance like *theboyhittheball* we would recognize only the upper unit (which is the sentence) and the lower unit (which is the sound), but in between we would be left with a problem, if not many. Fortunately, the scholars of English (as it happens to be English) have left spaces between the words. So we have the sequence: *the boy hit the ball.* To move further, we can use SUBSTITUTION, as in the sentence *John hit Mary.* To prove that *the boy* (and *a ball*) form one unit. Substitution again shows that *hit a ball* is also a unit (cf. John *came*). Finally, the upper unit as we know, is the whole sentence *the boy hit a ball.* This can be represented diagrammatically as follows:

(1)

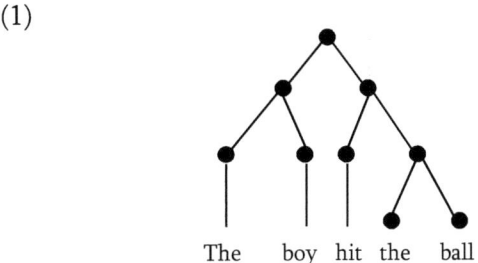

The boy hit the ball

We can say that although IC analysis is very explicit, it is rather limited as it does not draw any GENERALIZATION about language. (Soams & Perlmutter, 1979) Suppose now we started from top to bottom instead of bottom upwards. We would obtain what follows:

(2)

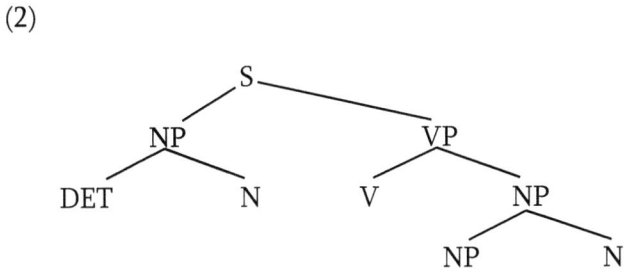

This will generate:

a. The boy hit a ball, and
b. The boy hit the ball, and
c. A boy hit a ball, and
d. A boy hit the ball, and
e. A boy hit a boy etc.

So we can see the merits of this new approach known as PHRASE STRUCTURE GRAMMAR (or the mathematical way of dealing with sentences which is much richer).

Now a piece of terminology seems necessary:

(3)

a. ( ): the item inside the parentheses is optional, as in: the (*old*) man - *old* is optional. This is in terms of acceptability.

b. [ ]: the items included in the square brackets form a unit like [*the old man*] which is a noun phrase.

c. { }: the items included in the braces form a paradigm or table of substitution as in:

$$\left\{ \begin{array}{l} \text{He} \\ \text{The boy} \\ \text{John} \end{array} \right\}$$

d. → stands for a phrase structure rule.

e. ⇒ stands for a transformation.

What we have established so far is the internal structure of the sentence *the boy hit a ball*, or indeed the generative system for all the simple, declarative affirmative (KERNEL) sentences of English (at least). It is called a TREE diagram, or PHRASE

MARKER (P-MARKER for short). It actually has two alternatives, the LABELLED BRACKETING as in (4):

(4) [s[NP[Det the][N boy]]] [VP[V hit][NP[Det a][N ball]]]]

and PHRASE STRUCTURE RULES[1]:

(5) S   →   NP - VP

    VP →   V - NP

    NP →   Det - N

    V   →   hit

    N   →   boy, ball

    Det →   the, a

3. Transformational Grammar

Now phrase structure grammar (PS grammar for short) itself is limited. It cannot possibly generate/link all the sentences of English. It especially faces problems such as DISCONTINUITY as in the sentence: *In God, we trust.* (in the Dollar). We know intuitively that in fact it is: *we trust in God* and likewise in the sentence: *what are you looking at that woman like that for, boy?* (Griffiths, Black Like Me) we know intuitively that *what... for* form one unit which is *why.*

PS grammar also faces the problems of DIFFERENCE between sentences (known as PARAPHRASE) as in the following paradigm:

(6)

a. The Moors defeated the Spaniards.

b. The Spaniards were defeated by the Moors.

c. It was the Moors who defeated the Spaniards.

d. The Moors' defeat of the Spaniards (was total).

e. I expected the Moors to defeat the Spaniards.

f. They defeated them.

Another problem faced by PS grammar (a semantic one this time) is AMBIGUITY². The noun phrase *old men and women* has two meanings, either: *old men and old women* (the second occurrence of the adjective *old* having been deleted) or *old men and any women*.

Finally, PS grammar faces the problem of SIMILARITY. Some sentences like *John is easy to please* and *John is eager to please* seem to have exactly the same surface structure namely NP, V, Adj. and S. But we know intuitively that the first sentence means something roughly like [*it is easy - someone pleases John*], whereas the second one means [*John is eager - John pleases someone*].

All these problems are solved by another grammatical rule called TRANSFORMATION. There were indeed many transformations in the early TG literature.

To take but one transformation, PASSIVE for instance, we need two main stages known as STRUCTURAL DESCRIPTION and STRUCTURAL CHANGE, as follows:

(7)

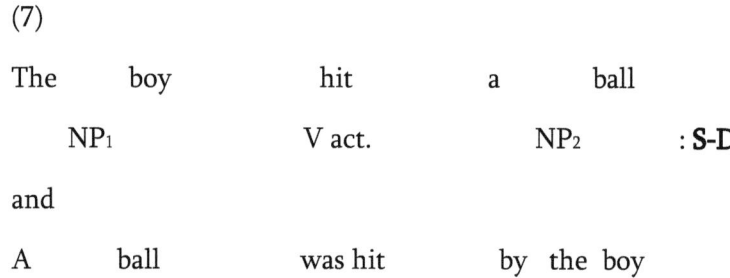

NP₂   V pas.   by   NP₁   : **S-C**

Three conclusions can be drawn about the first version of T.G.:

1. PS rules generate KERNEL sentences which are by definition simple, declarative and affirmative.

2. Transformations, unlike PS rules, are CONTEXT-SENSITIVE. They work according to the logical formula IF... THEN. For instance, you cannot have passive S-C unless you have its S-D.

3. Finally, transformations are by definition MEANING PRESERING[3]. They affect the form but not the meaning of sentences. (Chomsky 1957)

Notes

1. Furthermore, those categories happen to have RECURSIVE properties. That is NPs can include other NPs within them. For instance the NP *The man who ran the Marathon* contains within it the NP *the Marathon*. So we have an infinite class of structures because of this recursive property.

2. *The chicken are ready to eat* has got two deep structures; either *the chicken are ready to be eaten by someone,* or *the chicken are ready to eat the grains*, say.

3. This is open to debate, consider *not many arrows hit the target / the target was not hit by many arrows.*

4. Standard Theory

4.1. Phrase Structure Rules & Lexicon

Let us now see to what extent the PS rules suggested by Chomsky in his first book *Syntactic Structures* (1957) can handle the following sentence:

(1) *Sincerity may frighten the boy.*

(2) a. S   →   NP - VP

   b. VP   →   V - NP

   c. NP   →   Det - N

   d. V   →   frighten

   e. N   →   sincerity

   f. Det →   the

(3)

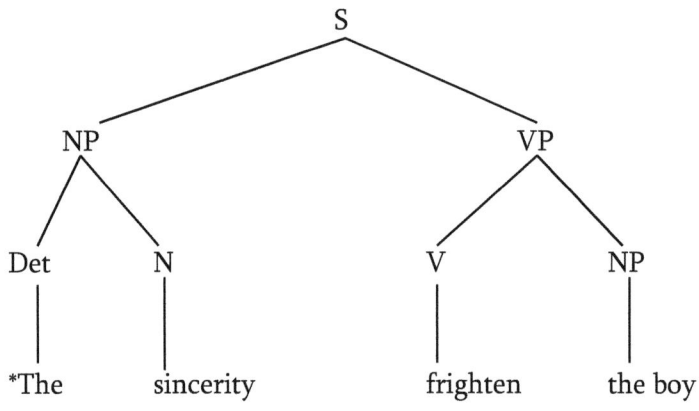

We notice above that the application of the above PS rules have left some problems and residues. For instance, the problem of tense is pending a solution and cannot be solved until we insert an Aux. node as follows:

(4)   S → NP - Aux - VP

Another problem concerns the idiosyncrasy of the English sequence [Det + N] in which [+abstract] Nouns do not take the definite article. The above P-Marker will also generate * the *sincerity frighten boy* or * *the boy frightened sincerity.* Notice that the PS rules above have not respected the "personality" of the verb *frighten* in many ways. The solution suggested by the STANDARD THEORY is to draw a categorical distinction between the first three PS rules suggested by the first version (enriched with Aux.) and the last three.

The difference is that the first three rules expand ABSTRACT SYMBOLS into abstract symbols; whereas the second set of rules expands symbols into actual WORDS of the language: S → NP-Aux-VP vs. V → frighten. The last three rules have been extensively developed in the Standard Theory and became the LEXICON. The latter first of all tells you that *boy* and *sincerity* are NOUNS (as a CATEGORY). This is largely similar to the traditional parts of speech but does not stop at that. It accounts also for their morphology. It divides the words (called FORMATIVES) into LEXICAL formatives like *table, follow, cat, above, etc.,* and GRAMMATICAL formatives like -s, -ed. Second, the lexicon gives you information about the SUBCATEGORIZATION of the formatives. SO verbs like *come, see, give, have (I have my car repaired every six months)* are INTRANSITIVE, TRANSITIVE, DITRANSITIVE and CAUSATIVE respectively (and can also mean eat). Thirdly, the lexicon includes semantic information known as SELECTIONAL RESTRICTIONS (a controversial point). Consider the following paradigm:

(5)

a. *He frightened

b. *He frightened sincerity

c. * He frightened the table

d. He frightened the boy

The first sentence is ungrammatical, because it does not respect the subcategorization of the verb frighten (a transitive verb). The second does respect its subcategorization but in the wrong way by giving it an abstract object. The third does indeed give it an [- abstract] object but [- animate]. The last sentence gives it the right object which is [+ animate] ([+ human] being redundant).

4.2. Transformations

After the PS RULES and THE LEXICON, the Standard Theory suggests a second type of rules; namely TRANSFORMATIONS.

(6)

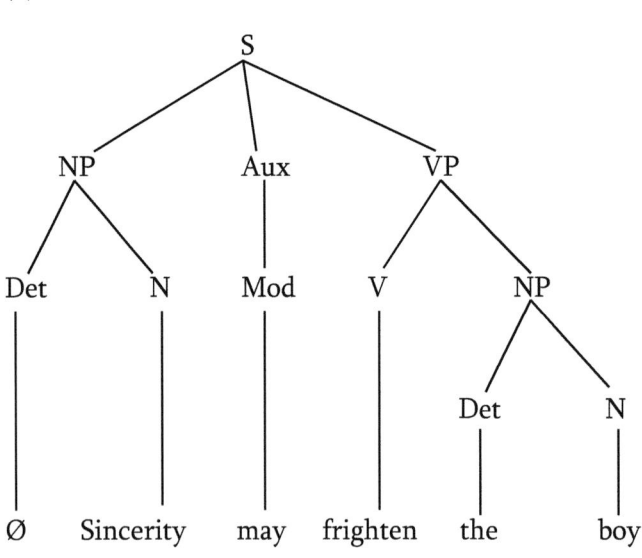

Consider again the sentence *sincerity frightened the boy*. If we apply the PS rules suggested in (4) we will obtain.

(7)

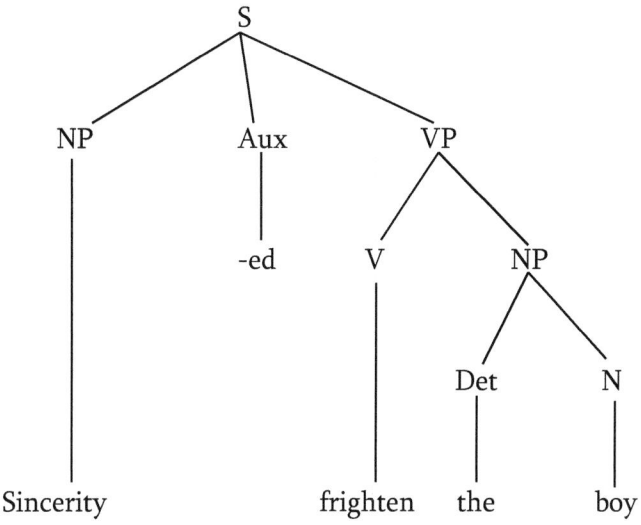

We are left with the grammatical formative *-ed* (past tense marker) on the left of the verb; a representation which is undesirable (this hypothesis has strong empirical support though, from emphasis *I did work hard!* and question *did you work hard?*).

Chomsky suggests the application of an OBLIGATORY transformation called AFFIX HOPPING to (7) to yield (8):

(8) Sincerity frighten-ed the boy.

Suppose now we had a verb like *took*, this model suggests that we would start with an abstract string called occasionally DEEP STRUCTURE like *he -ed take the book*, but even after affix hopping has applied, we will be left with a problem of morphology: take *-ed*. To solve it we would need another obligatory transformation called MORPHOPHONEMICS:

(9) take+ed → took

Consider now the difference between morphophonemics and passive:

(10)

a. The boy hit+ed the ball ⇒ The boy hit the ball

and

b. The boy hit the ball ⇒ the ball was hit (by the boy)

As far as acceptability is concerned, the second sentence namely *the boy hit the ball* does not need any transformation and hence PASSIVE is an OPTIONAL transformation; whereas AFFIX HOPPING (morphophonemics in general) is OBLIGATORY (for acceptability considerations).

4.3. Transformational Cycle

Finally some sentences need a transformational CYCLE. Consider the utterance *serve yourself, won't you?* Let us try and suggest the following deep structure for it and all the way from that to the surface structure:

(11) you will serve you

A series of transformations is needed to reach the surface structure: QUESTION-TAG, IMPERATIVE DELETION and REFLEXIVIZATION. What does each one of these three transformations say? TAG: "Copy Aux then make it negative and copy the subject to its right". IMPERATIVE: "delete the subject and Aux". REFLEXIVIZATION: "turn the second NP into a reflexive pronoun in case of COREFERENCE".

Let us apply these transformations as suggested.

(12) a. TAG: you will serve you ⇒ you will serve you, won't you?

b. IMP: you will serve you, won't you ⇒ serve you, won't you?

Ahaa! We had no first NP to apply our reflexivization to. We have committed a BLEEDING destruction/absence of SD to borrow Kayne's terminology. We probably need to leave imperative until the end. We have to respect a certain order called CYCLE: 1. tag, 2. reflexive, 3. imperative, or TRAFFIC RULES as Chomsky* (1965) calls them. (You don't put the shoes before the socks, do you?) (For further analysis of the transformational cycle see the excellent book by Kayne *French Syntax the Transformational Cycle* e.g. *cela le fera téléphoner à ses parents*)

5. Pronominalization

Langacker (1969) suggests some constraints on pronominalization (transformation); he states: "Our goal is to answer the following question about English: under what conditions can a definite noun phrase NP^a be used to pronominalize an identical noun phrase NP^p?" and his answer: "We are now in a position to state the major restriction on pronominalization quite succinctly: NP^a may pronominalize NP^p unless (1) NP^p precedes NP^a; and (2) NP^p commands NP^a." e.g. **Ralph** *is much more intelligent than* **he** *looks*.

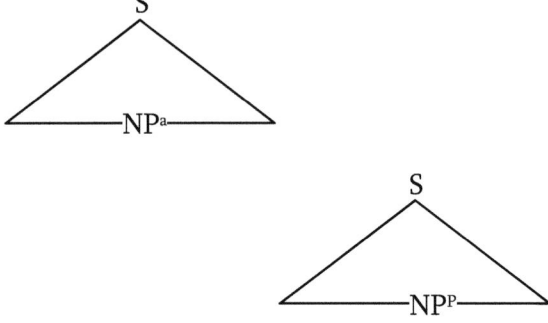

6. Conclusions

a. The STANDARD THEORY suggests an ABSTRACT initial form called DEEP STRUCTURE.

b. It draws a distinction between OBLIGATORY and OPTIONAL transformations.

c. When more than one transformation is needed, we must respect a certain order called CYCLE.

d. Paradoxically, the seventies saw the crucial need for constraining the power of transformations, e.g. John Ross's A-Over-A and Islands. This is on the one hand; on the other hand there was a shift this time to deal with semantic problems, namely reference. (see Langacker's "on pronominalization and the chain of command." (1969).

Notes

"Consider the sentence *John seems to be liked by Mary* which, in theory, would itself derive from a deep structure *It seems Mary likes John*, then we would have two transformations: first Passive would move *John* to the initial position of the embedded sentence *It seems John is liked by Mary*. Then a rule of Raising would raise the subject John to the initial position of the matrix sentence, yielding *John seems to be liked by Mary*. (Chomsky 1972)

(For Minimalist Program, see Ben Rochd El. Forthcoming)

LANGACKER'S COGNITIVE GRAMMAR

Langacker states: 'Given that language effects the pairing of forms and meanings, to what extent is their connection motivated rather than arbitrary? The classic principle of *l'arbitraire du signe* (de Saussure, 1916) is simplistic even in the case of lexemes, and fares even worse if extended to grammar. A basic tenet of Cognitive Grammar (Langacker 1987, 1991, 2008) is that lexicon, grammar, and even discourse reside in a continuum of form-meaning pairings. In all but the simplest expressions, iconicity proves to be a major factor.'

For Langacker, consciousness is the state of a man who is not asleep or in a coma. The linguistic knowledge of such a man can be describable. Although there is a spectrum of what a man can achieve without being fully aware of actions such as walking, driving, etc. on the other hand, the process of vision, hearing... consciousness is not fully accessible to scientific description...

Cognition consists of correspondences between entities e.g. *seats* and *guests* in a *dinner party* for instance recognizing the same person met on different occasions, (a certain identity/identification), or the identity of a shape in different spots, in which case we easily perform the mental act of transportation.

The 'delicacy' of our analysis depends on our specific objectives. Global correspondence is sufficient for these purposes while others require local correspondence. In cognitive grammar, there are correspondences: symbolic, categorical and syntagmatic.

In the study of idioms, we find that the correspondence of literal meaning with metaphysical meaning is an expression of semantic intention. This global relationship is also decomposable into local relations. The extent of discrepancy is quite variable in an idiom such as: *the cat is out of the bag*, the conflict in specification between [cat] and [information] is blatant. It is hard to perceive any similarities: [bag], however, bears the natural and salient relation to [concealment] and the difference between [out] and [out-of] is minor (spatial vs. abstract domain).

According to Jonathan Miller, the implications of 'what is said' are often at odds with its literal meaning. The turn of voice and context settle the point instead of putting a direct request, it is usually couched in the form of an announcement, which is inoffensive, e.g. 'I wonder if you could pass on the salt' is in fact a camouflage request for the salt.

Synecdoche is another figure of speech in which the part is used for the whole e.g. *Inkasara l-kursiy* (Arabic) 'The chair broke.' Literally, this means that the whole 'chair broke' in fact the leg of the chair broke only.

The Taoist poet said:

> *Into a soul absolutely free*
>
> *From thoughts and emotions,*
>
> *Even the tiger finds no room*
>
> *To insert its fierce claws.*

> *One and the same breeze passes*
>
> *Over the pines on the mountain*

And the oak trees in the valley;

And why do they give different notes?

No thinking, no reflecting,

Perfect emptiness;

Yet therein something moves,

Following its own course.

The eye sees it,

But no hands can take hold of it –

The moon in the stream.

Clouds and mists,

They are midair transformations;

Above them eternally shine the son and the moon.

Victory is for the one,

Even before the combat,

Who has no thought of himself,

Abiding in the no-mind-ness of Great Origin.

(Bruce Lee 1975)

The word *Soul* stands for 'a man' as part used to denote the whole. A man being 'a soul' and 'a body.' This is also another example of synecdoche.

As a professional Chomskian linguist, having just started to read the works of Ronald Langacker, I may be biased, as it seems to me that *cognitive grammar* goes against Chomsky's 'autonomous syntax hypothesis' and Saussure's '*arbiraire du signe*' theory. It further reminds me of traditional notional grammar and some Arab grammarians who saw meaning in every syllable and every phoneme of the Arabic language. (Ibn Jinni)

CHILD LANGUAGE

(In remembrance of Patrick Griffiths)

1. Overview

Language can be studied from different perspectives namely its origin, structure and use. It is also very interesting to try and understand how it is acquired by the infant. Patrick Griffiths worked much on different aspects of language studies, namely psycholinguistics, semantics, pragmatics, etc. In his article "The Communicative Functions of Children' Single-Word Speech", he focuses on language in use by children.

Quoting philosopher Searle' taxonomy, Griffiths tries to account for the different types of child's ILLOCUTIONARY ACTS. He also relies on the dichotomy REFERRING and PREDICTING (i.e. reference and predication). He draws the analogy of a sports commentator who would be most boring in one way and quite interesting in another, comparing comments about phonology and syntax on the one hand and comments about semantics on the other. He favors the latter. Young children are assumed to use language – like the adults – to achieve Illocutionary Acts. They seem to have at hand all of the adult's linguistic arsenal i.e. speech acts: *Negation*, *question*, *affirmation*, in rudimentary form shall we say?

ILLOCUTIONARY ACTS are what people do when they talk. These are the most obvious acts such as *greetings*, *promising*, *re-*

questing together with the acts of REFERRING and PREDICATING. According to Searle: 'ILLOCUTIONARY ACTS are the basic units of linguistic communication'. Austin (1962), who pioneered the study of ILLOCUTIONARY ACTS, surmised that there are several hundreds of different kinds of speech acts: the ones in italics above plus *naming, knighting, betting, welcoming*, etc.

While talking, the speaker has the purpose of performing PERLOCUTIONARY ACTS i.e. *inspiring, dissuading*. They have no conventional connections with linguistic expressions: what will *inspire* one person will *alarm* another and *bore* a third. With the barest minimum of control over pronunciation, children begin to use language communicatively at the age of about 9 months.

2. Searle's Taxonomy

Given that there may be as many as a thousand different kinds of illocutionary acts, it will help to have them sorted out into a smaller number of more general classes. Searle (1975a) has attempted such a classification:

-Expressives

-Directives

-Commissives

-Assertives

-Declarations

ILLOCUTIONARY ACTS IN THE HOLOPHRASE PERIOD

Griffiths' (1985) motive for the major heading of this section, Illocutionary acts in the holophrase period was to restrict the focus principally to this archetypal segment of the 'single-word period', though he occasionally, especially in connection with questions and assertives, transgresses its upper bound.

The talk of the 'single-*word* stage' in child language development is a little misleading, though it is undoubtedly a convenient designation for the period that extends from (approximately) 9 months ('first word') to (approximately) 18 months (first productive concatenation of words–initially only two at a time–within a single tone unit.)

For the first half of the 'single-word stage' the child's utterances are Holophrases rather than words. A holophrase usually has the length of a (short) adult word and may be modeled on an adult word pattern but has communicative functions comparable to a whole sentence uttered by an adult.

Griffiths gives several examples from child speech to illustrate Searle's taxonomy. The first problem is defining the nature of children's words. A child of $18^{1/2}$ months made his first two-word sentences; he first said *fan* then, after a pause, *on*. His mother reported that he evidently expected the fan to be turned on after naming the *OBJECT* first.

Greenfield and Smith (1979) observed Geenfield's son, Matthew, and another child, named Nicky. They classified their utterances according to (syntactically relevant) semantic roles? Other authors accepted both idiosyncratic child forms and ones that appeared to be modeled on adult words, but not easily relatable to them. In fact, the child and his caretakers are continuously engaged in the joint construction of a communication system. The use of negation '*No*' occurs usually to accompany desired, but forbidden, 'action', as opposed to 'entity'. From his early sixteenth month child Matthew used *no* 'to reject situational events'.

Two further types of illocutionary acts should be mentioned here: VOCATIVES and QUESTIONS. Vocatives are the simplest conceivable kind of directive. They simply summon the addressee's attention to the speaker. Let us call this type a DEICTIC VOCATIVE (pointing to oneself by means of speech sounds). Questions seem to be absent from the holophrase period.

Child Nicky pointed to things, saying *ada* with the intonation of *What's that?* Seeming to express the need to be told a *name*. He showed his intention when he went ahead trying to change the non-linguistic world to match a proposition.

An assertive commits the speaker to the truth of a proposition. The proposition could be supplied by someone else's *Yes-No* question. The child does not bother about agreement between his/her answers and the facts. How else could a younger child, limited to 'one word at a time', have a proposition in play for a truth commitment? The younger child talks almost exclusively in relation to the 'here and now'. In one of the examples provided by D, we are told that when J's mother points to a picture of a dog and asks *What's this?* J responded *bow wow*.

As far as Declarations are concerned, Griffiths states that, 'the only example known to me that fits this category is supplied by D (1975): *mama* with a falling terminal intonation contour was used in circumstances where the child merely labeled his mother or some doll as the mother…' This would seem to be the case of a declaration that some entity shall have a particular name (and/or role?)

In summary, Griffiths states, 'Searle's *expressive* and *directive* categories each seem to be well-represented and internally differentiated in the holophrase period. *Assertives* may be present towards the end of the period, but *commissives* and *declarations* are at that time apparently still absent. *Questions* are largely un-attested in holophrase speech, notwithstanding the fact that Searle includes them in the directive category. The component act or *referring* grows out of the most basic type of attention-directing, the *deictic vocative*. During the holophrase period, referring increases in sophistication: initially there is only *plain deixis*; then there is *quasi-reference*; what I (Griffiths) have been calling true *reference* appears. These developments in referring are reflected in corresponding successive refinements in the performance of illocutionary acts. For example, initially, directives can only be deictic ('Do That', 'Give Me That'); later they can be quasi-referential ('give me food/feed me'); finally the child becomes capable of referential directives ('Get Mama for me'). The arrival of the component act of *predicating* –a prerequisite for the making of assertive illocutionary acts – heralds the end of the holophrase period.

3. Patrick Griffiths

[Describing his own very rich career, PAT as we (his students) used to call him, or *Patlik* (as a Japanese girl used to call him), he says:

"On a baffling introduction to English literature that I underwent a long time ago, one of the lecturers used up class hours by strutting as he proclaimed that "poetry is an athletic art performed with the vocal limb." No hints were given as to what that meant, but his example persuaded me that being baffling is a waste of students' and teachers' time; so I have aimed since then to be clear (even if it takes more words). The reward has been students who talk back, raise problems and ask lots of questions, which has pushed me into trying harder to understand my own subject: the workings of language.

Linguistics and psychology were my bachelor degree majors. I wrote an honors dissertation on second language learners' implicit knowledge of English grammar as revealed by their comprehension errors and successes. One branch of my mind got a start in educational linguistics from me taking a part-time job as a writer of exercises for students of English as a second language. I learnt statistics on another job.

For my doctoral degree at Edinburgh University, the focus was on word meanings and how young children begin to attach meanings to words. I had part-time teaching jobs in the university and also worked on two child language research projects.

My first full-time university teaching post was at the University of York (the one in the UK), where I taught courses in semantics, child language, psycholinguistics and the structure of English. I also learnt a great deal about language in education from being the anchor person for a course that put students in schools for a whole year, in the UK and elsewhere in the world, to discover through practical involvement how English is learnt and used.

After that I spent six years in Fiji, teaching applied linguistics, semantics, psycholinguistics and the structure of English at the international University of the South Pacific (which serves twelve Pacific island countries that, between them, have 200 different languages).

For 18 months back in the UK, at York St John University, I taught on TESOL (Teaching of English to Speakers of Other Languages), psycholinguistics and history of linguistics courses. Then I spent five years at Beppu University, in a beautiful part of Japan, where I ran English language and linguistics courses, including a TEFL certificate programme. Since then I have taught semantics and pragmatics at York St John, and have worked hard on trying to learn to read Japanese.

PSYCHOLINGUISTICS

(In remembrance of Jonathan Miller)

The amazing organization of the *bee* colony is obviously based on its no less amazing 'language'. The latter system has challenged the researchers for a long time, until German Karl Von Frisch of Munich University found the solution to that mystery after spending thirty years of patient (read painful!) research and observation (Benvenist 1966). Still, the so-called bee language seems dramatically limited when compared to child language. Those 'buzz speakers' have no way of asking questions, contradicting, criticizing or making a conversation. By contrast, the human infant has a large vocabulary repertoire amounting to thousands of words that he can draw on effortlessly whenever the situation requires. The language of human *babies* is much more versatile and creative than any communicative system found elsewhere. Man is unique.

'Any progress toward this goal will deepen a problem for the biological science that is already far from trivial: how can a system such as human Language arise in the mind-brain, or for that matter, in the organic world, in which one seems *not to find* anything like the basic properties of human language?' (Chomsky 1997, p.2)

Earlier, in the 1950s, Chomsky had already startled the academic world by stating that the child comes to the world knowing about language long before he knew which one he had to speak. He is endowed with some congenital machinery that makes it possible for him but not, say for a dog or an ape to speak a language.

'The fact about languages... we don't really learn any more than we learn to have arms. It just grows. You can't help it. You speak to your child in an environment where language is being used and that child has no more choice whether to weigh five pounds or something or decide not to eat. It can't decide not to learn that language, because learning language is just a process that the brain goes through under certain conditions. It is a process of growth not a process of what people call learning. The system grows in certain ways because of the way it is built.' (Chomsky 1970)

In the many books and articles that Chomsky wrote ever since *Syntactic Structures* (1957), Chomsky drew attention to facts about language which are quite inconsistent with the idea of program learning and still less imitating the utterances which the child has heard in the first years of his life. (You see for one thing) the child becomes a competent user of language long before he has heard enough of it. And in any case the sort of things the child says when it first begins talking is so unlike what it has heard from its mother that the idea of being a straightforward playback is obviously nonsense.

It becomes increasingly obvious that in learning to speak, the child uses something that it has already received from the hands of nature. (God's Truth)

In early Greece, Plato had suggested that birth was not the beginning of life but intervened half-way in the life of the individual. This idea was powerful enough to influence Chomsky as it did with English romantic poet Wordsworth more than 2000 years later:

> *Our birth is but a sleep and forgetting:*
>
> *The soul that rises with us, our life's Star,*
>
> *Hath had elsewhere its setting,*
>
> *And cometh from afar:*
>
> *Not in entire forgetfulness,*
>
> *And not in utter nakedness,*
>
> *But trailing clouds of glory do we come*
>
> *From God, who is our home!*
>
> (William Wordsworth)

In fact this verse of Wordsworth is a paraphrase of what Plato had written when he insisted that the birth of a man is not the beginning but the middle of his existence. During the course of his antenatal life, Plato assumes that an individual is endowed with fundamental thoughts of the universe and unlike the embodied person that he will eventually become, spiritually predecessor... He did not perceive the world through the five senses but by grasping it directly.

Plato represented birth itself as some mid-life crisis i.e. a catastrophe, the trauma of which causes the unfortunate refugee to half forget whatever he has previously known. He insisted that the survivor of that cataclysm somehow retained mysteriously residues of his previous knowledge and that (the faint of) that half-forgotten wisdom which accounted for otherwise inexplicable speed with which the growing child recognized the esoteric truths of maths and geometry.

Although Plato's idea was no longer associated with the notion of previous existence, the emphasis which was given to the internal virtues of the mind had a very powerful impact on structure studies of language. Both English and French scholars now stressed the underlying of human language and by pointing out the fact that there appears to be no limit to the power of the mind. They implied all human beings were endowed with some congenital organization which was particularly favorable to the acquisition of creative speech.

In the late 50's, Chomsky was to revive this tradition and establish it in the context of modern biological and psychological thought. 'The problem was why does it take so long to acquire language? It was thought that instilling habit by training was the manner in which language was acquired.'

In the name of what came to be known as behaviorism, psychologists systematically abstained from using the concept of 'mind' and concentrated instead on the observable conduct of experimental animals to try to show administration of calculated punishments and of rearwards. Behaviorist psychologists had claimed that language, as well as any other aspects of human behavior, was based on automatic stimulus-response processes. As a behaviorist, American psychologist Skinner saw language in those terms. [cf. Bloomfield's Jack and Jill]. For instance, I feel thirsty, I ask for water and a glass of water is brought to me. I drink and my mind records the connection between the word 'water' and the feeling of satisfaction. The synapse connection is established.

By opposition, the *mentalists* related language or language competence for Chomsky, to the unknown structure of the mind. Chomsky thinks that the deep structure of languages is universal and language learning is an innate human capacity. So linguistics and psychology were bound to meet. The linguistic skills of perception and production both spoken and written forms are all controlled by the mind and therefore covered by branches of psychological studies. The child produces something he is very unlikely to hear from the adults. He comes to the world preprogrammed with the linguistic endowment.

Langue consists of a set of *linguistic features* on the three levels: syntax, semantics and phonetics. At the phonetic level, the Phonetic Features are those that distinguish words such as *bat* and *pat*. They are crucial. The helpless infant may distinguish them although he has no way of telling the difference they can make in the world of the adults. Another crucial contrast in the adult's language is the one found between consonant and vowel. Still, the infant's uttering is expressed through an open airway.

The baby goes through fixed stages which are babbling, one word stage, two words stage, telegraphic style, etc. from *babbling* the first words start to spring. During that stage he reiterates the same closures and utters the same syllables over and over again *baba*, *mama*, *nana*, and so forth. He has no way of alternating different consonants. What he hears from adults' speech are just unfragmented stretches of sounds. This is by no means enough to imitate, and is much unlike what he hears. Then comes the alternation phrase and *words* start to emerge. The alternation of closures will give *baba*.

Speech is a continuous *stream of sounds* you just have to listen to a foreign language sentences to notice. There are obvious word boundaries *Kenya hakuna matata*. Words alone are not enough. *Syntax* comes into play combining words together and assigning semantic roles to each constituent. The infant is in fact a welcome guest and takes part in the conversation. The child works by over *generalizations*. He would utter things such he worked, he hammered. Then he will learn the exceptions one by one. *I runned-I goed-it broked.* Parents may start panicking. But the child will speak later more discriminately.

Language learning is a puzzle for most researchers. Some have suggested the behaviorist answer, others the mentalist one. Most parents have been most excited when they noticed the emergence of the first words from babble. Then the first sentences excite the pride of the parents. This has involved two processes, natural capability and social support. It is amazing!

In 1970 a rather tragic case was reported to the *Child Welfare Authorities* in Loss Angeles. Susan, a 13 year old girl, was shuttered in a cottage and no one spoke to her. If she made the slight attempt to speak, she was punished. The problem with her was the psychological trauma besides the deprivation of any linguistic input. Sympathetic treatment led her to acquire a vocabulary but her grammar was dire.

That the child has a native endowment does not mean that he can acquire language in a complete absence of conversation input. But his natural competence is the one that allows him to seize on the first language he hears and make a meal of it. This may explain the rapidity and uniformity in child language acquisition.

At a deeper level than deep structure, you find the psychological *Universal Grammar (UG)* for short, where all languages are suspiciously alike. This is why they can be translated into one another. It is like a political constitution. It does not state what to do but rather sets limits to what can be done, 'you can't do that, you can't do that either! It is like the visual system. You only need a few hints to say that this is a man or an animal. We do not learn that any more than we learn how to eat. It's a labor saving device. We make sense of a very impoverished data.

An adult trying to learn *Japanese* (an OSV language lacking movement transformation, cf. Comrie 1999, p.55) would scorn the idea of having a universal grammar which showed that the differences between languages were trivial and that they *all were cut to the same pattern??*

Deep structure is responsible for disambiguating phrases and sentences such as:

The old men and women

They were visiting firemen.

The boy saw the man with the telescope.

Transformations operate on the deep structure to yield the surface structure. Some of these are passive, relativization, question, particle movement, etc. as in:

The ball was hit by the boy.

The old man in the corner is waiting for the bus.

Who is in the room?

Particle Movement Transformation

In a phrase marker where there is a V followed immediately by a verbal particle followed immediately by a noun phrase, the particle can be moved to the immediate right-hand side of the noun phrase.

This is why we can have:

He hooked up the word in the dictionary.

He hooked the word up in the dictionary.

Both are grammatical. Sometimes this transformation is obligatory as shown below:

*He looked up it in the dictionary.

He looked it up in the dictionary.

He gouged his eyes out.

He gouged out his eyes. ()

Transformations apply at the phonetic level as well, as in the case of spirantization, 'in segmental phonology... intervocalic spirantization and vowel reduction are natural and simple processes that derive, say, Hebrew *ganvu* "they stole" from underlying g-nB' (Chomsky 1997, p. 224). Or as in Palestine for *Filistin*.

The mind is responsible of expressing thought into language. But unfortunately some people have lost this beautiful capability either by a disorder caused by a problem of the vocal cords or by an injury to the brain areas responsible for language, known as a *Stroke*. The disorder in language can find new channels. It is not through the adequate expulsion of air through the vocal tract, it is the hand gestures and pantomime that take over.

By presenting language as an arbitrary Sign System (vs. onomatopoeia), Swiss Ferdinand de Saussure never meant a humpty dumpty system. Rather he meant that language is similar to the chess game; there is no observable link between the pieces and what they refer to in the game. There is no obvious or natural link between the form and the function of the pieces on the game table. Rather it is the set of contrasts that give unambiguously the game its sense.

Chomsky is also responsible for drawing an important dichotomy distinction between competence and performance (to shadow somehow Saussure's *langue/parole*). These stand respectively for the potential capability of the speaker and the realizations of this faculty on different occasions. The first one is finite while the other is infinite.

'From now on, I will consider language to be a finite set of rules that generates an infinite set of sentences.' () all sentences have to obey the rules to be acceptable (*).

Vocabulary is a necessary condition for coherent speech but not sufficient. Grammar and word-order play a no less important role. In fact grammar may be the key to understanding the semantic roles of each noun phrase in the following:

John killed Mary.

Is not saying the same thing as:

Mary killed John.

Although they consist of the same words.

The Enlightenment is a period in 18th c. Europe in which philosophers tried to run before they could walk. They raised the fundamental question about 'man's nature?' classifying individuals with anatomical certainty; they wanted to establish the 'Science of Man'. They suggested phrenology for the brain map. They tried to localize the different functions of the brain.

In 1860, French doctor Paul Broca contributed an amazing advance to neurological science by discovering brain lateralization and speech pathology. He discovered that the lower front lobe of the left hemisphere was responsible for the production of speech. This he found with the autopsy of one of his diseased patients. Boca's aphasics did not suffer from any damage to their vocal cords; rather they suffered from injuries to the part of the brain that is responsible for recruiting the speech muscles.

In 1874, Austrian Wernicke reported nine cases of patients that reflected Boca's aphasia. They were fluent speakers but only uttered incoherent nonsense. Wernicke's patients did not comprehend the difference between 'come' and 'go'. Wernicke's patient, a lady, uttered 'I am 1803. That's me! Yes! Yes! Yes!' an injury to the further back of the left side hindered the Information Flow Diagram. While Boca's aphasia has to do with the motor function of the vocal tract, Wernicke's aphasics will have problems recognizing a clock. A Wernicke's aphasic was asked, 'Is it a sieve? A dish you eat your dinner off? The answer was, 'Yes!' 'Does it tell the time?' 'Is 4 O'clock or 3 O'clock?' 'Yes!' the answer was again.

Conduction Aphasia is yet another language pathology. Its patients would have difficulty uttering words such as 'statistical', or sentences such as 'they heard him on the radio' or again 'they bought fruits, vegetables and a bottle of milk'. It would be rendered as 'something to eat!'

According to Jackson, aphasic people go through the regressive path of evolution to the level of lower animal: loosing more and more of the human endowments. (Broca)

Wittgenstein was one of the Cambridge philosophers. He had a crucial role in shifting the focus of philosophy from metaphysical questions to language. The language game is designed not only to express one's thoughts but also, and more importantly, 'to do things with words!' An utterance can express an order, a wish, a prayer. Speech Acts are defined as, 'in speaking, we choose: whether to make a statement or ask a question, whether to generalize or particularize, whether to repeat or add something new, whether or not to intrude our own judgment, and so on.' (Lyons, 1970)

To understand the language unconscious machinery child language, aphasia and speech acts may give the key. Some hypotheses have been formulated on that black box full of mysteries. Some of the questions are: 'What are the formal (mathematical) rules and properties? What does this program run on?'

The problem we are facing with language is how to unravel the unconscious language machinery secrets. 'In spite of the vast accumulation of knowledge, scholars are still unable to propose a biological theory of language – a formal model of a brain mechanism consistent with the physiology described by Lenneberg and the type of psychological data...

(Jonathan Miller)

CONCLUSION

In this book [WORDS - Traditions in Linguistics (Revised)], we have tried to trace the ideas and theories of imminent philosophers, philologists, and linguists, of the past and the present, and the evolution of different trends and schools from earlier ones to the modern times. Every scholar (or group of scholars) has tried their best to answer the question, 'what is LANGUAGE?' They have looked at it from different angles and perspectives; its nature, its structure, its history, its sociology, philosophy and psychology.

LANGUAGE is basically the same miracle for every people; therefore, it should have the same basic definition. Instead, theories and schools of thought and linguistics differ and they do enormously.

According to Fassi-Fehri (1982), 'linguistic relations can be determined as grammaticality, ambiguity, synonymy, entailment, analycity, contradiction, etc. To give adequate answers to these problems, we needed to fix a set of methods, principles and constrains so as to give an appropriate description of languages. But soon, each linguistic trend or school diverges in a special way and takes its unique specific axioms and methods not shared by others.'

According to Popper, one cannot expect finality in any scientific investigation. Of many competing theories, we can at best determine which one is better. "Lenneberg has reported a wealth of biological data relevant to language. These range from studies of the peripheral anatomy of the speech organs to the correlations between symptoms of language dissolution and injury to particular brain areas; from the genetic substance of certain inherited language disorders to the physiological correlates of vocalization, and from the functional organization of the central nervous system to the structural, chemical and electrophysiological changes which define the maturation of brain during the period of the first-language acquisition. But in spite of the vast accumulation of knowledge, scholars are still unable to propose a biological theory of language – a formal model of a brain mechanism consistent with the physiology described by Lenneberg and the type of psychological data summarized in the chapters by Campbell and Wales (pp.242-60) and Johnson – Laird (pp.261-70). Advances in knowledge have only shown even wider areas of ignorance" (Lyons 1970, p.241).

GLOSSARY

APHASIA

A disorder of the central nervous system with loss of speech ability.

BEHAVIORISM

A school of psychology that regards objective external observation as the only valid subject for study.

BERBER

A member of a Caucasian Muslim people of n Africa, the language of this people.

BONAFONTE

Italian Linguist who espoused the view that language change is a matter of 'taste and fashion' rather than 'scientific laws.'

BRAIN

Organ responsible for Sensory-Motor-Cognitive functions.

BROCA

French neurologist, responsible for the discovery of the Broca's Area (see Wernicke's Area).

CHINESE TRADITION

'Of all the living languages of the world, Chinese has the longest unbroken recorded history, with texts in the language dating from as long as 35 centuries, and there is reason to believe that the art of writing in china may go many centuries further back than this.' (Wang 1995)

CICERO (43 BC)

Roman orator and politician.

COGNITIVE

The mental act or process by which knowledge is acquired.

COGNITIVISTS

Langacker 'cognitive grammar' is a highly innovative theory of linguistic structure that has been developed and progressively articulated since 1976. In stark contrast to modular approaches, it regards language as an integral facet of cognition, and grammar as being inherently meaningful. It presupposes a 'conceptionalist' account of linguistic semantics that properly recognises our capacity for construing the same conceived situation in alternate ways. With an appropriate view of meaning, all grammatical elements are reasonably attributed some kind of conceptual import. Grammar is thus considered 'symbolic' in nature: it reduces to the structuring and symbolization of conceptual content.

COMPETENCE

Unconscious knowledge (vs. Behaviorism) that helps you recognize that certain pairs of words rhyme, that certain phrases are synonyms of other phrases, that some sentences are ungrammatical. (Chomsky)

DEDUCTION

The process of reasoning leading to a conclusion from a set of premises.

DIGLOSSIA

A sociolinguistic term referring to a situation in which two forms of a language co-occur.

DONATUS (4th c. AD)

There was serious study of Latin as it is the 'original' language of the New Testament. The most influential roman grammarian of the 4th c. was A. Donatus who wrote two grammars: *Ars Minor* and *Ars Major*. The first deals with word classes whereas the second book deals with morphology, syntax and a prescriptive grammar of Latin.

EMPIRICISM

The doctrine that all knowledge derives from experience.

EPISTEMOLOGY

Epistemology is usually defined as the theory of knowledge, esp. the critical study of its validity, methods, and scope (from GK epistèmè: knowledge)

ETYMOLOGY

The study of the roots and development of words.

FORMAL LINGUISTICS

It is the study of grammar of the development of theories as to how language works and is organized. Formal linguistics compares grammars of different languages, and by identifying and studying the elements common among them, seeks to discover the most efficient way to describe language in general. The ultimate goal is "Universal Grammar" – the development of a theory to explain how the human brain processes language.

Within formal linguistics, there are three main schools of thought: traditional, structural and transformational.

Traditional grammar is the one that is most familiar to the majority of us. A typical definition in traditional grammar is 'a noun is a person, place, or thing.' 'adjective clause', noun clause', 'complements', etc. Structural linguistics, a principally American phenomenon of the 1940's. In linguistics, it was principally concerned with phonology, morphology and syntax. Transformational-generative approach to the description of language was introduced in 1957 by Chomsky.

GENERATION

A term derived from mathematics, and introduced by Chomsky to refer to the set of formal rules that project a finite set of sentences upon the infinite set of sentences that constitute a language.

GERMAN TRADITION

The German language belongs to the Germanic family (Gleason). It is mainly spoken in central Europe. It is one of the major languages of the world. It is inflected with 4 cases (nominative, accusative, genitive and dative), has 3 genders, two numbers, and strong and weak verbs. Amongst its most famous linguists and philologists are Paul, Schleicher and Grimm. Amongst its most famous figures in linguistics and universal culture is Johan Wolfgang (Von) Goethe (1749-1832) a poet, playwright and literary theorist amongst his most famous works is *Faust* and *Eastern Divan*.

GESTALT

Gestalt psychology is a system of thought that regards all mental phenomena as being arranged in patterns or structures perceived as a whole and not merely as the sum of their parts.

GRIMM

He is the responsible for the principle of consonantal shifts in pronunciation known as Grimm's Law 1822.

HALLIDAY M.

His systemic functional grammar is pursued widely in the UK, Canada, Australia, China and Japan.

HOUSEHOLDER'S LABELS

Hocus-pocus vs. 'God's Truth' (Sampson, p.72)

HYMES

American scholar who developed a pragmatic approach called the ethnography of speaking.

IBN JANAH (990-1050)

His Arabic name Abu Lwalid Mawan or Rabbi Jonah is the most prominent Andalusia Hebrew grammarian of the middle ages. He studied syntax, lexicon and biblical exegesis. He started his carrier as a physician, devout Jew he devoted much of attention to biblical Hebrew so as to give the interpretation of that holy nook a solid linguistic foundation. He left many books including al-mustalah amazingly written in Arabic like all his other books. He was in conflict over verb morphology with another scholars such as Judah ben David Ḥayyuj, the founder of scientific Hebrew grammar. This led him to bitter confrontation with the fans and students of the latter. This was recorded in his book Kitab at-tanqih. In its first part ie Kitab al-luma, ibn Ibn Janāḥ dealt with Hebrew grammar, including discussions about parts of speech, prefixes and declensions. His contribution to syntax was paramount. The second part of his bok Tanqih Ibn Janah dealt with (verb) roots and showed their rage and showed the nuances of word roots. His approach based on illustrative examples, he made extensive comparisons of Hebrew and Arabic and thereby managed to clarify the meaning of many (Semitic) words. His comments helped biblical the exegesis up to now with many obscure biblical passages.

INDUCTION

A process of reasoning that reaches a conclusion from a number of experiences.

I.P.A.

An abbreviation of International Phonetic Alphabet.

JEROME (420 AD)

Christian monk and scholar, producer of the vulgate.

LATERAL

To produce a lateral, 'make this sound [l], then keep your mouth in that position and *draw air inwards*; make small changes in the position of the tip and blade of the tongue until you can feel that cold air is hitting the tongue at the very centre of the alveolar ridge, not further forward and not further back' p.41., 'most languages have a sound like English [l], at least before vowels, and this can be used in such words as /liːv/ leave, /laːst/ last, /lʊk/ look… Some languages, however (Japanese, for instance), do not have a satisfactory [l] sound, and such students must be very careful to make a firm contact of the tongue-tip and the sides of the blade with the alveolar ridge. If this is difficult for you, try biting the tongue-tip firmly between top and bottom teeth; this will make a central obstruction and the air will be forced to pass over the sides of the tongue. In passing to the vowel the tongue-tip is removed from the alveolar ridge quite suddenly and the sound ends sharply; it may help to put in a very quick d-sound between the [l] and the following vowel /ldi:v/ leave, etc... the [l] sound in English, whether it is dark or clear, must be a lateral, it must have a firm central obstruction and air escaping over the sides of the tongue' (O'Connor, J.D. 1966. *Better English Pronunciation*, CUP, Cambridge, p.41, p.70)

LEXEME

A term referring to the common, abstract element which underlies the various forms of a word, e.g. *go*, *goes*, *going*, *gone*, *went* would be all forms of the same underlying lexeme GO.

LINGUA FRANCA

A common language for different speech communities living in the same country, such as English in Nigeria.

LOGICAL FORM

The concept of logical form has two meanings, one is the philosophical tradition, and one in theoretical linguistics (see above).

LUTHER (1483-1546)

German leader of reformation, translated the Bible into German.

MANDARIN CHINESE

This language relies on ideograms. It goes as far as 3500 BC, longest record (see Confucius) of 'human speech'.

MARTINET (1908-1999)

French linguist influenced by Prague school.

MENTALISM

The doctrine that mind is the fundamental reality.

MNEUMONIC

Aiding or meant to aid one's memory.

MONGOLIAN

'In a Mongolian dialect (Trubetzkoy, 1939, p.17) frontness of vowels 'expresses' sex: back vowels in men's speech correspond to central vowels in women's speech...' (Sampson 1980, p. 111)

MORPHEME

The minimum distinctive unit of grammar.

ONTOLOGY

The branch of philosophy that deals with existence and the nature of being.

PAVLOV (1849-1936)

Soviet physiologist. His study of conditioned reflexes in dogs influenced behaviorism. He also made important contributions to the study of digestion.

PHONEME

The minimum unit of the sound system.

PHONETICS

That science that studies the properties of human sound-making.

PIDGIN

A language made up of elements belonging to two or more languages.

POETICS

A term used to refer to the linguistic applications to poetry (Roman Jacobson).

PORT ROYAL (16th c.)

Originally, Port Royal was a famous Cistercian Covent in the *vallée des chevreuses* southwest of Paris that launched a number of culturally important institutions. The Arnauld family became its patron. Antoine Arnold's book *Grammaire logique et générale*, was probably the most outstanding linguistic work of port royal tradition.

P.S. RULES

Phrase structure rules are those finite mathematical rules (discussed in Chomsky's *Syntactic Structures* (1957)), which are capable of generating an infinite number of sentences.

PRAGMATICS

One of the three divisions of semiotics.

RATIONALISM

The doctrine that knowledge is acquired by reason.

R.P. (RECEIVED PRONUNCIATION)

The regionally neutral accent of British English (also called Queen's English).

RELATIVES

Relative clauses are either restrictive such as:

Many students who major in mathematics find employment with computer companies.

Or descriptive (holding a comma) such as:

Arkansas, which became a state in 1836, was earlier a part of Louisiana.

SANSKRIT

An ancient language of India. It is the oldest recorded member of the Indic branch of the Indo-European family of languages (See Panini 4th c. BC). From PIE descended Sanskrit, Latin, Greek, Proto-Germanic, and various other known hypothesized ancient languages... who invented alphabet in 700 BC? (Koener, p.73)

SAPIR EDWARD

A leader in American structural linguistics; he was one of the first who explored the relations between language studies and anthropology. His methodology had strong influence on all his successors.

SCIENCE

A discipline based on four successive/ordered foundations: Observation, Hypothesis, Experiment [cf. Japanese Dr. Takaki] and finally Theory. Still scientific induction is merely based on approximation, in spite of attempts of being consistent, exhaustive and (not) absolute!

SCOPE PRINCIPLE

See Scope of quantifiers, e.g. Not all children play all games.

STYLISTICS

A branch of linguistics which studies the different choices and figures of speech. It is usually held by linguists that style is the proper of the individual (another fingerprint similar to voice). This is to say that each person has his own specific way of thinking and therefore his own way of speaking and writing.

These probably reflect the particular mind structure of each individual.

We could perhaps try to defend this view by taking into consideration the different popularities earned by different writers. The readers tend to recognize particular features to every writer's work and this is what makes Goethe Goethe and an unknown writer unknown.

Language is more than its phonetic, psychological and social dimensions. It is perhaps the most subtle facet of human life. It is more than a mere instrument of communication. It is a living creature in its own right. It can reach the horizons of art in literature. Its sounds can surpass the normal harmony of music. Its patterns are sculpture and architecture. It relives man's heart, shapes his ideas and makes the whole universe speak to him.

SPE

The Sound Pattern of English (frequently referred to as SPE) is a 1968 work on English phonology achieved by Noam Chomsky and Morris Halle. It presents a view of phonology as a separate subsystem of linguistic analysis separated from the other components of grammar. It is basically transformational in outlook moving from phonemic form to the ultimate phonetic form.

TAGMEMICS

This school (SIL) applies – emic ideas to phonology, grammar and vocabulary, i.e. task small movement. Pike argues that linguistic methods are able to identify the functionally important (-emic) features of any aspect of behavior out of the objective (-etc.) data which the analyst is presented with.

TRANSFORMATION

A transformation is a grammatical operation that links a deep structure to a surface structure. (Chomsky, 1965)

U.G.

A term used in generative grammar, to refer to the common properties of all human languages.

WHORF

Son of immigrants to the Massachusetts. He was a brilliant amateur of linguistics and chemical engineering. He worked as a fire inspector in the Connecticut.

BIBLIOGRAPHY

Al-Nassir. A. 1993. *Sibawayh the Phonologist.* Kegan Paul Inter. London & NY.

Abdel Ghany, M. 1981. *Government-Binding in Classical Arabic.* PhD. Austin. Texas University.

Al-Waer . 1980. "An Interview with Noam Chomsky." MIT. Cambridge. Mass.

Aoun, J. 1986. *A Grammar of Anaphora.* MIT. Cambridge. Mass.

Ben Rochd, E. 1982. *French Passive.* MA, York.

Ben Rochd, E. 1990. *Pronominalization in Classical Arabic.* PhD, Dublin.

Ben Rochd, E. 1991a. 'Aoun's Generalised Binding & Arabic Evidence'. *Revue de la faculté des lettres.* Numero 2. Oujda.

Ben Rochd, E. 1991c. ' Barriers and Arabic'. *Linguistica Communicatio III.*

Ben Rochd, E. 1993. *Schools of Linguistics.* Takafia. Casablanca. [AR]

Ben Rochd, E. 1994a. *Generative Grammar.* Takafia. Oujda.

Ben Rochd, E. 1994b. *Linguistic Theory in America.* Jadida. Casablanca. [AR]

Ben Rochd, E. 1995. *Arabic and Semantics.* Ms. University of Washington.

Ben Rochd, E. 1995b. *Form & Meaning –Face to Face: Non-Concatenation, Logical Form & Idiomatics*. University of British Columbia. Canada.

Ben Rochd, E. 1997a. 'X-bar, DP, Occam's Razor and LF in Arabic'. *Bulletin of the Faculty of Humanities and Social Sciences*. Vol. 20, University of Qatar.

Ben Rochd, E. 1997b. *The Evolution of Transformational Grammar*. Oriental. Oujda.

Ben Rochd, E. 1999a. *Arabic & Logical Form*. Dechra. Casablanca.

Ben Rochd, E. 1999b. "Arabic, Origins, Structure and Most Outstanding Grammarian: Sibawaihi". *Revue de la Faculte des Lettres*. Numero 7. Oujda.

Ben Rochd, E. 2001. "Sibawaihi, The Syntactician". *Revue de la Faculte des Lettres*. Numero 4. Beni Mellal.

Ben Rochd, E. 2020 a. *Sibawihi's Transformational Grammar*. Books-on-Demand.

Ben Rochd, E. 2020 b. *Generative Grammar*. Books-on-Demand.

Ben Rochd, E. 2020 c. *Evolution of Chomsky's Transformational Grammar*. Books-on-Demand.

Beneveniste, E. 1966. *Problème de la linguistique générale*, Galimard, Paris.

Bittner, M & K. Hale. 1993. 'Ergavity', ms, MIT. Cambridge. Mass.

Bloomfield, L. 1993. *Language*, Holt, New York.

Borer, H. 1983. *Parametric Syntax*, Foris, Dordrecht.

Bresnan, J. 1970a. "An Argument against Pronominalization," *Linguistics Inquiry* 1, 122-23.

Bruce Lee. 1975. *Tao of Jeetkunedo*. Ohara Publication. Burbank. California.

Brusse, W. 1974. *Klasse Transitivitat Valenz*, Fink, Munich.

Carter, M. 1968. *A Study of Sibawaihi's Principles of Grammatical Analysis*. PhD. Oxford.

Chomsky, N. 1957. *Syntactic Structures*. Mouton. The Hague.

Chomsky, N. 1965. *Aspects of the Theory of Syntax*. Mouton. The Hague.

Chomky N. and M. Halle. 1968. <u>The Sound Pattern of English</u>. Harper & Row. New York.

Chomsky 1972a. *Studies on Semantics in Generative Grammar*. Mouton.The Hague.

Chomsky, N. 1972b. *Language & Mind*, Harcourt Brace & Joeavich.

Chomsky, N. 1977. "On Wh-Movement," *Formal Syntax*, Academic Press, New York.

Chomsky, N. 1981. *Lectures on Government & Binding*. Foris. Dordrecht.

Chomsky, N. 1982. *Some Concepts & Consequences of the Theory of Government and Binding*. MIT. Cambridge. Mass.

Chomsky, N. 1986. *Barriers*. MIT. Cambridge. Mass.

Chomsky, N. 1988. *Language & Problems of Knowledge.*, MIT. Cambridge. Mass.

Chomsky, N. 1994. "Bare Phrase Structures", ms. MIT. Cambridge. Mass.

Chomsky, N. 1997. *The Minimalist Program*. MIT. Cambridge. Mass.

Chomsky, N. 2020. "The Delphic Oracle: Her message for today".

Comrie, B. 1989 *Language Universals & Linguistic Typology*, Blackwell, Oxford.

Comrie, B. 1990. 'On the Importance of Arabic for General Linguistic Theory'. *Perspectives on Arabic Linguistics*. University of Southern California.

Crystal, D. 1985. *A Dictionary of Linguistics and Phonetics*. Blackwell. Oxford.

Emonds, J. 1976. *A Transformational Approach to English Syntax*. Academic Press. New York.

Emonds, J. 1987. "Parts of Speech in Generative Grammar," *Linguistic Analysis* 17, 1-42.

Er-Ramadani, Y. 2003. Acquiring Tarifit-Berber. Aksant. Tilburg.

Evans, T. 1972. "Chomsky", *Brain Research Association*, London.

Fassi-Fihri, A. 1989. "Agreement, Incorporation, Pleonastics, " ms. MIT. Cambridge. Mass.

Fiengo, R. 1977. "Trace Theory," *Linguistic Inquiry* 8, 35-61.

Fromkin, V. & R. Rodman. 1983. *An Introduction to Language*. Holt-Saunders, New York.

Gazar, G. 1979. "Unbounded Dependencies & Coordinate Structures," *Linguistic Inquiry,* 12, 155-184.

Gleason, H. 1969. *An Introduction to Descriptive Linguistics*. Holt-Saunders. New York.

Griffiths, P. 1985. "The Communicative Functions Of Children's Single-Word Speech." *Children's Single-Word Speech*. John Wiley and Sons, Ltd.

Ibn Jinni. 1952. *Al-Khasa'is*. Cairo

Kayne, R.1975. *French Syntax: the Transformational Cycle*. MIT. Cambridge. Mass.

Khalaily S. 1997. *One Syntax for All Categories*. H.I.L. The Hague.

Koerner E.F. & R.E. Asher. 1995. *Concise History of Language Sciences*. Pergamon. Cambridge.

Kremers J.M. 2003. *The Arabic Noun Phrase A Minimalist Approach*. MA. Katholieke Universiteit.

Langacker, R. W. 1969. 'On Pronominalization and the Chain of Command'. Reibel & Schane.

Langacker, R. W. 1995 'Cognitive Grammar' in *Concise History of the Language Sciences from the Sumerians to the Cognitivists*. Pergamon. Cambridge. Mass.

Langacker, R.W. 2020. "Structure, Iconicity, and Access." Ms University of California, San Diego.

Lyons, J. 1970 . *New Horizons in Linguistics*. Penguin. Middlesex.

Lyons, J. 1981. *Language and Linguistics*. CUP. Cambridge.

McCarthy, J. 1979. *Formal Problems in Semitic Phonology and Morphology*, PhD. MIT. Cambridge. Mass.

Newmeyer, F. 1980. *Linguistic Theory in America*. New York. Academic Press. New York.

O'Connor, J.D. 1966. *Better English Pronunciation*. CUP. Cambridge.

Ouhalla, J. 1988. *The Syntax of Head Movement. A Study of Berber*, PhD, University College London.

Ouhalla, J. 1989. "Clitic Movement and the ECP." *Lingua 79, 165-215.*

Ouhalla, J. 1994. "Verb Movement and Word Order in Arabic." *Lightfoot & Hornstein. CUP* . Cambridge.

Ouhalla, J. 2002. "The Structure and Logical Form of Negative Sentences in Arabic". *Themes in Arabic and Hebrew Syntax*, (ed. Jamal Ouhalla & Ur Shlonsky, Kluwer, Dordrecht.

Ouhalla, J. 2004. "Semitic Relatives." *Linguistic Inquiry*, Vol. 35, N 2, 288-300. MIT. Cambridge. Mass.

Palmer F. 1982. Grammar. Penguin. Middlesex.

Pickthall M. *The Meaning of the Glorious Koran*. Mentor. NY.

Radford, A. 1981. *Transformational Syntax*. CUP. Cambridge.

Radford, A. 1988. *Transformational Grammar*. CUP. Cambridge.

Robins, R H. 1967. *A Short History of Linguistics*. Longmans. London.

Sampson, G. 1980. *Schools of Linguistics*. Hutchinson. London.

Wright, W. 1979. *A Grammar of the Arabic Language*. CUP. Cambridge.

Walker, K. 1944. *Meaning and Purpose*. Jonathan. London.

Gott Dank Sein!